HONG KONG
State of Mind

*37 views of a city
that doesn't blink*

Jason Y. Ng

HONG KONG State of Mind

The author would like to thank Lee Po Ng for the 40 magnificent illustrations featured in this volume, Natalie Lo and Tak Chi Lin for appearing on the cover, Blacksmith Books for its editorial support and his blog followers whose staunch support has made this book possible.

First published 2010
Second printing 2011
Third printing 2013

ISBN 978-988-19003-1-9
Copyright © 2010 Jason Y. Ng
Cover photograph and illustrations © 2010 Jason Y. Ng
www.jasonyng.com

Published by Blacksmith Books
5th Floor, 24 Hollywood Road, Central, Hong Kong
www.blacksmithbooks.com

Cover design and photography by Jason Y. Ng
Illustrations by Lee Po Ng

*For my parents,
who have given their all
to their five children*

HONG KONG
State of Mind

Silver cities rise
   The morning lights
The streets that meet them
   And sirens call them on with a song

– CARLY SIMON,
Let the River Run

The beautiful city,
   The city of hurried and sparkling waters!
The city of spires and masts!
   The city nested in bays!
My city!

– WALT WHITMAN,
Mannahatta

Contents

Introduction 11
About the Illustrator. 13

Part 1 – The People We See

Rhapsody on Pedder. 16
All Downhill from There 20
The Butcher's Atonement 24
Tutelage of the Tutored 30
Kowloon Complex. 33
Ah Gah and The Hill. 37
Laws of Nature 41
My Pet Peeves 46
Why Must All Our Minibuses Be Yellow? 52
A Little Bay No More 58
A Matter of Taste 62
An Aw-some Day. 66
The Dark History of Sedan Chairs 70
Hong Kong State of Mind 74
I Died Three Saturdays Ago. 82

Part 2 – The Things We Do

Pink Elephants On Our Streets 88
To Eat or Not to Eat 94
What's in a Cup. 99

Total Eclipse of the Mind................... 105

The Secrets of Self-Preservation............. 110

Confessions of a News Junkie............... 115

Daily Conundrum.......................... 121

Riding out the Tsunami.................... 125

Department Store Culture.................. 132

In Sickness or in Health................... 137

Flip-flops Culture......................... 145

Christmas in Hong Kong................... 148

Part 3 – The Places We Go

Tokyo Impressions........................ 156

A Tale of Three Cities..................... 160

Paradise of the Blind 173

Nikko Revisited........................... 178

City Without Skyscrapers.................. 182

I Heart NY 188

Seoul Searching........................... 196

Bangkok Story............................ 204

Island Escapade 214

Tokyo Impressions – A Year Later........... 217

Introduction

My brother Kelvin and I disagree on just about everything. Politics, favorite movies, how much to tip at restaurants and what to do with rude taxi drivers. That's what brothers do. That's why we enjoy each other's company.

And so when I first told him the idea of turning my blog into a book, Kelvin, true to form, served up a dose of reality check. "Who would want to read about stuff they already know?" he asked rather rhetorically. Indeed, much of what I write is based on everyday life in Hong Kong – the people we see, the things we do and the places we go – things that have long seeped into the subconscious and no longer alarm us or bother us.

"And you don't even write in Chinese!" Kelvin continued his bubble-bursting routine. But he does have a point. Even though every Hong Konger grows up speaking Cantonese (the city's *lingua franca*) at home and learning English at school, the latter remains ever elusive, ever feared. To most adults, reading an English book is about as exciting as getting a colonoscopy or watching your aunt Sarah's wedding video in slow motion.

But if two wrongs can make a right, then this book is it. When the stories we know are told in a different language, even the familiar and the mundane can spring to life. That's the same reason every foreign film set in Hong Kong, from *The World of Suzie Wong* to *Batman: The Dark Knight*, never fails to fill us with anticipation and trepidation. Deep down we always wonder how we are perceived by the outside world and whether we measure up. This book is meant to be that foreign movie, made by someone who is at once an outsider looking in and an insider looking out.

Hong Kong is a remarkable place. It is a place of possibilities, contradictions and endless quirks that, like a lover's whispers, make us smile from the bottom of our hearts. Our city deserves a book to celebrate its splendors and poke fun at its flaws. It deserves hundreds of them. With that, I am certain, even Kelvin would agree.

Jason Y. Ng
Pokfulam, 2010

About the Illustrator

Born in the town of Toishan, Guangdong, Lee Po Ng (伍里甫) followed his mother to Hong Kong during the Chinese Civil War. Ng quit school at the age of 15 to become an apprentice to a local painter and spent the next four decades working as a freelance cartoonist and illustrator under the aliases Sze-ma Yu (司馬瑜) and Yut Dor (一多).

In the 1960s, Lee Po Ng tried his hand at editing and went on to launch a daily newspaper with a group of like-minded friends. But refusing to trade his paintbrushes for a pen, Ng continued to tread the unbeaten path of a newspaper illustrator. His artistic career peaked in the 1980s during the heyday of the print media, contributing to as many as 15 newspapers, among which *Ming Pao* (明報) and the *Sing Tao Daily* (星島日報) are still in circulation today. Ng now resides in Toronto, Canada with his family. He splits his time between teaching art and practicing calligraphy and traditional ink and wash painting in his home studio.

Lee Po Ng is the author's father.

Part 1
The People We See

畢打街狂想曲

Rhapsody on Pedder

It was an unseasonably cold November afternoon. I finished my workout at California Fitness and hurried back to the office. I walked down the precipitous Wyndham Street, where dense traffic from Midlevels collected and emptied onto Queen's Road Central. The cacophony of car horns and audible traffic signals for the blind reached a deafening crescendo, drawing everyone's attention to the busy crosswalk that marked the start of Pedder Street. There, pedestrians built up along the curb and stared unseeing at their mirror image on the opposite side. Double-decker buses and delivery trucks pushed forward in every direction and shook the ground like a wildebeest migration. Dispassionate traffic lights changed at even intervals, trapping and releasing machines and humans competing for speed. The opening bars of George Gershwin's *Rhapsody in Blue* started to ring in my head. It was lunch time in Central.

The busy intersection where Pedder Street meets Des Voeux Road Central

Outside Marks & Spencer, a homeless woman lay prostrate on the sidewalk, her hair wrapped in wrung-up plastic bags and her body a cocoon of sullied blankets. Either a family tragedy or financial ruin must have pushed her over the edge, for the woman spent the day flapping her arms on the sidewalk mumbling to herself, slowly becoming a fixture on the Central street scene. But she got company today. A stern policeman stood over the forlorn woman and shouted down at her in gruff Cantonese. His words might have been drowned out by street noises, but his message was clear: she was to disappear from Central forever. Pedestrians watched with momentary interest, though deep down inside they all agreed that there was no room for unsightly roadblocks in our city, much less on prime real estate like the Pedder and Queen's intersection. To think that her shenanigans could go on unchallenged, the homeless woman was not only mentally ill, she was also hopelessly naïve.

As I continued my saunter down Pedder Street, I breached a wall of people queuing up at a roadside cash machine. Outside the Citibank branch at the Des Voeux Road Central intersection, a bullhorn was blasting pre-recorded grievances at passers-by. A quartet of elderly women, dressed all in white, held large placards above their heads, leveling blistering accusations in both Chinese and English: "Citibank, Bloodsuckers!", "Crooks!", "Citibank swindled us!" Next to them an armed security guard watched with abandon. The protestors were among the thousands of retirees who lost their life savings in the notorious Lehman Brothers mini-bonds. They were the reluctant poster children of risky financial products and the first casualties of a global crisis hitting home. Left to their own devices, how long would it take before they all wound up next to the homeless woman outside Marks & Spencer? In a city devoid of a social safety net, aren't we all just one bad investment decision away from ending up on the street?

Across the street from Citibank, a very different scene unfolded. Outside the glittering Louis Vuitton store at the Landmark, a line of eager shoppers waited in single file just to get in. They were the ubiquitous "free individual travelers" (自由行) from Mainland China under the auspices of a government scheme that relaxed travel restrictions for private citizens and had given a welcome boost to neighboring economies. Men with beer guts and bad shoes, women with clumsy makeup and dated hairdos – hardly the kind of clientele the French fashion label had in mind – could not wait to pay five figures for a canvas bag and turn themselves into walking billboards for the monogram logo. Inside the store, shoppers preened their plumage of new wealth, their wallets matched only by the loudness of their voices. The big spenders sized up every item on display, seemingly oblivious to the predicament of the placard-holders across the street. Or were they? Perhaps all that binge spending carried a far deeper meaning. If the mini-bond investors personified the transience of wealth, then perhaps every thousand-dollar bill the shoppers doled out echoed exactly that same sentiment: what is here today may be gone tomorrow. So let's just live in the present and leave the future to philosophers and fortune-tellers. Materialism is bliss and hedonism the only way of life.

The traffic lights turned green and I crossed the tram-tracked Des Voeux Road toward Worldwide Plaza. I hiked up to the elevated walkway traversing the ten-lane Connaught Road Central before disappearing into one of the Exchange Square towers. Just two city-blocks long, Pedder Street is a caricature of our city's inexhaustible energy and dreary alienation, ever accentuated in times of anxiety and pessimism.

走
下
波

All Downhill from There

A few weeks ago I attended a business meeting with a roomful of people, all native Hong Kong Chinese, from various investment banks. During lunch at a nearby Italian restaurant, I was flanked on my right by Patrick, a junior analyst fresh out of university, and on my left by his boss Terrence, a managing director in his late 40s. Terry was balding, pudgy and rather talkative.

I had barely sat down at the lunch table when Terry fired his first question at me: "Your name is Jason, right? What school did you go to?" Patrick turned his head and stared at me, eagerly awaiting an answer.

Vexed by the irrelevance and irreverence of the stranger's probe, I replied as politely as I could, "I went to law school in Toronto, but that was many years ago."

"No, I mean the high school you attended," Terry interjected. "Young Patrick here went to St. Joseph's on Kennedy Road," the forty-something senior banker continued with a half joke, "but that's because he couldn't get into the other school down the street!" That "other school," by the way, was St. Paul's Co-educational College, one of the top secondary schools in Hong Kong, also on Kennedy Road.

"They are both very good, aren't they?" I offered a truce. Out of the corner of my eye, I spotted a class ring engraved with the letters S.P.C.C. on Terry's left hand, just inches from his glistening Rolex.

*   *   *

What happened during that awkward lunch wasn't an isolated incident. In our Bizarro World, which secondary school a person attends may tell you a lot about his background, pedigree and even social status. That's why the subject of high school comes up frequently in schmoozing events, whether it is a business lunch or Friday night happy hours, as a way for strangers to size each other up before a pecking order can be established. It's a Hong Kong thing.

Local secondary schools here, confusingly called "colleges" when they are not, are divided into different tiers known as "bands." It is a form of government-sanctioned discrimination that smacks of the Indian caste system. At the top are the so-called "band one" schools that accept the brightest students and offer them the best teachers and other resources. Among these elite schools are the two Diocesan Schools and LaSalle College in Kowloon Tong and St. Paul's Co-educational and St. Joseph's in Mid-levels. They are the Oxbridge and the Ivy League of secondary schools. Because top-tier schools are typically located in affluent areas, and because students living in a particular school district stand a much better chance of getting admitted under the current placement scheme, secondary schools have become a proxy for socio-economic class in a stratified society like ours. The labeling effect doesn't apply to universities: the fact that an applicant lives five minutes away from, say, Baptist University, gives him absolutely no advantage over others in faraway districts. Besides, we had only two universities and a handful of community colleges until the 1990s, and college degrees weren't nearly as commonplace a generation ago as they are today. All that has made local secondary schools one of the more universal measures of where we stand and how we fare in the eyes of society.

Diocesan Boys' School in upscale Kowloon Tong

No matter how special these hoity-toity secondary schools feel about themselves, they are, let's face it, *just* secondary schools. How sad is it for a society to take so seriously what most reasonable people would consider ancient history? And how very lame is it for grown men and women to still be bragging about their *alma mater* years or even decades later? But none of that seems to register with the local population. Obsessive parents map out their children's career paths from the age of three and pour their life savings into an overpriced apartment to get within a desired school district. And once the teenagers make it through those iron school gates, they find themselves caught up in endless interschool rivalries that border on the absurd and continue well into adulthood, such as the one played out so brazenly between Terry and Patrick at the lunch table. When it comes to that one chapter in our lives, we seem utterly incapable of letting go of the past.

Our inability and unwillingness to let go is best captured by those dreadful high school reunions organized by alumni with way too much time on their hands. "Reunions" is an euphemism for networking events where insurance salesmen, real estate brokers and financial advisers shamelessly hit up old classmates for business. It is remarkable that, of all the people that come into and out of our lives, high school buddies always end up our most reliable social and professional connections. And despite all the life experiences we accumulate over the years, few leave as deep a mark as those blurry moments in the classroom and on the playground. Now that we are out in the real world, as the daily grind of life bears down on us mercilessly – slaving away in the office till 11pm and beating back pressure from family and friends to get married and have children – we all look back on those innocent, wholesome high school days with a bittersweet smile. We can't help but wonder, deep in our hearts, whether life had already peaked in our teenage years and it's all downhill from that point on. Maybe that's why we find it so hard to let go.

屠夫的救贖

The Butcher's Atonement

The other night my niece asked me to tell her the story of Tiananmen Square. My avuncular instincts kicked into high gear and I made up a story more suited for juvenile consumption.

Once a upon a time in a land far far away, an old butcher ran a humble meat shop. One hot summer's night, he got into a heated argument with his sons over the way he managed his struggling business. In a fit of rage, the impetuous father reached for his cleaver and went on a bloody rampage. Shocked by his own monstrosity, the man frantically buried the bodies and vowed to be a better father to his remaining children. As the years passed, the butcher shop prospered and the family grew. Still, any discussion of that fateful summer's night remained taboo. Convinced that he would never be forgiven, the old man resigned himself to waiting out the generation who witnessed his murderous acts. With each passing day, as memories thinned and denial thickened, the old butcher's chance of atonement ebbed away like a receding tide.

*   *   *

The Tiananmen Square Massacre, or more delicately referred to as the "June 4 Incident" in this part of the world, was the most senseless chapter in Chinese history since the Cultural Revolution. On June 3, 1989, if Beijing citizens had to make a list of things they thought would never happen, their government using the bluntest arrows in their authoritarian quiver by sending in the tanks in the dead of night and opening fire on unarmed demonstrators still asleep in their tents would have been right at the top of their list.

The chain of events that led up to the bloody crackdown was more surreal than a Dali painting. Not two months before June 4, exuberant students camped out in the heart of the capital city, shouting rousing slogans one moment and singing the *Internationale* the next. Two weeks before June 4, student leaders wearing headbands and pajamas sat side-by-side with party chiefs in the Great Hall of the People exchanging ideas on political reform. Such fatal naiveté! How could anyone place even an ounce of trust in a regime utterly incapable of negotiation or compromise, or ever believe that lofty ideals would somehow move party seniors who took the slightest criticism as a personal affront? In the end, the student demonstrators got a lesson no textbook could teach them. And hundreds became part of a story they would never live to tell.

*Hundreds of Beijing University students camped out on
Tiananmen Square in summer 1989*

Twenty years later, Tiananmen Square was once again in a complete lock-down. Security had been heightened and armed police were everywhere. Determined to make the anniversary a national non-event, authorities summarily removed dissidents from the capital city and kept the less vocal ones under temporary house arrest. Twitter, Hotmail and Flickr had been blocked for a "national Internet service maintenance day."

But Beijing has little to worry about. June 4 is nothing but a historical blip for most Mainland Chinese. Young people born after the incident haven't even a chance to learn or hear anything about it, at least not through public discussions or school books. And in a country that boasts the fastest growing population of millionaires in the world, money speaks louder than ideology. Lured by the promise of a comfortable middle-class life, many opt for a foreign car and a big apartment over political reform that may or may not benefit them within their lifetime. These days, university students are busy applying to graduate schools in America and interviewing with multinational companies, in what many believe to be a modern reenactment of Goethe's tragic play *Faust*. From fearless idealists to unabashed pragmatists, the pendulum has swung to the other extreme in a single generation.

In Hong Kong, the only place on Chinese soil where free discussions of the massacre are possible, a couple of interesting preludes set the stage for the 20th anniversary. In April, Ayo Chan (陳一諤), the dorky know-nothing student president at the University of Hong Kong, outraged his colleagues at a campus forum when he suggested that the entire tragedy could have been avoided if the demonstrators had not behaved irrationally and provoked the Communist Party. Thankfully, fellow students acted swiftly to impeach the loose-tongued freshman before he moved on to the subject of the Holocaust and accused the Jews of taunting the Nazis.

Just two weeks ago, Chief Executive Donald Tsang told legislators that whatever happened in Beijing that day "happened a long time ago" and that the incident was better forgotten given all the prosperity China has brought us. And as if things weren't bad enough, the bow-tied bureaucrat kept on stressing that his view represented the opinion of every Hong Kong citizen. Politicians are well advised to speak cautiously, and if that's too hard to do, speak only for themselves. From university leader to government head, those who lack the maturity or conscience to separate facts from lies in the grown-up world should join my niece in learning the story of the old butcher. Learn it and remember it.

Earlier tonight I attended the candlelight vigil at Victoria Park. With teary eyes and a heavy heart, I put on a black-and-white outfit as if I were going to a dear friend's funeral. At the park, somber citizens occupied every occupiable space as far as the eye could see. To my left, a young couple held on to their infant fast asleep in the summer's heat. To my right, a sweaty teenager led two blind men negotiating the crowds with their walking sticks. Every one of us chanted pro-democracy slogans and strained to hear impassioned speeches drowned out by the chorus of cicadas singing loudly in the trees. Twenty years ago, demonstrators besieged Tiananmen Square to demand the vindication of ousted party chief Hu Yaobang (胡耀邦). Twenty years later, I found myself among 150,000 sitting in a peaceful protest demanding the vindication of those very demonstrators. Despite Hong Kong's many foibles and political anomalies, tonight our city was the collective conscience of the 1.3 billion Chinese people around the globe and a beacon of hope for a better China. I had never been more proud of being a part of this city.

*   *   *

If this were a fairy tale, my niece would thank me for the lovely bed-time story and fall sound asleep under her quilt embroidered with giraffes and zebras. But we don't live in a fairy tale. In reality, my nieces and nephews never asked me about Tiananmen Square and I never told them the story of the old butcher and his slaughtered children. Our next generation is either too young to be interested in politics or too busy with homework and exams. But how I want them to ask me what this anniversary really means! I want my next generation to know their country and its history, for how we remember our past defines who we are and how we live our future. Throughout the night, Rudyard Kipling's famous poem *Recessional* kept playing in my head. And on this 20th anniversary of one of the defining moments of my childhood, I dedicate these lines to my next generation.

> *The tumult and the shouting dies,*
> > *The captains and the kings depart.*
> *Still stands Thine ancient sacrifice,*
> > *An humble and a contrite heart.*
> *Lord God of Hosts, be with us yet,*
> > *Lest we forget - lest we forget!*

上了學生的一課

Tutelage of the Tutored

I have been teaching English in my spare time for several years now. I classified my students into two main groups. The first comprises mostly eleventh and twelfth graders who need help with their literature class. They tend to be children of well-to-do expatriates who have been plucked from faraway homes and placed in one of the handful of exclusive international schools in the city. As traumatic as their displacement has been, these young, porous minds quickly adapt as they bond with schoolmates who share similar experiences.

I work with a learning center in Central that supplies me with a steady flow of students. Corporate executives and their spouses, dissatisfied with their children's report cards and either too busy or unable to rectify the problem themselves, turn to the learning center for a hired hand. To many of these concerned parents, I am just another employee they hire to make their problems go away, giving me no qualms about charging them top rates and splitting it fifty-fifty with the center. The center, on the other hand, is placed in the unenviable position of having to deal with every antic of their demanding customers.

I spent many an evening in my home library preparing for class

But once I get past the parents' egos, it's all about timeless literature and the authors who created it. Watching my students go from "I don't know why I have to read this" to "okay, that was kind of interesting" makes sacrificing my Sunday mornings all worthwhile. It also gives me a perfect excuse to dust off my Shakespeare, Fitzgerald and Joyce and spend a quiet evening at home organizing my thoughts and parsing them into digestible doses for my students' consumption. In their eyes I see a reflection of myself back in those blurry high school days. And through my own voice I hear the words of my twelfth grade literature teacher Mr. Quinlivan, minus the lush Irish accent.

The other group of students I teach comprises everyday folks from a cross-section of society. They come in all ages, professions and aspirations, from a 19-year-old office clerk who wants to watch Hollywood movies without Chinese subtitles to a trio of hairdressers at a beauty salon seeking group lessons on how to communicate with foreign customers. These students are typically working adults who stopped learning and using English the day they stepped out of school. Few within this group have much extra cash to spare and I charge just enough to cover teaching materials.

Last weekend I took on a new student by referral. Flora has a keen interest in foreign cultures and loves reading English-language novels on her daily commute to work. At the start of our first class I asked Flora to give a three-minute introduction of herself, just so I could gauge her oral proficiency. My new student took a deep breath and a few seconds to collect her thoughts and, instead of gabbing about hobbies and favorite foods, began telling the life story of a woman who was born with a physical disability but had recently gained mobility through surgery. Suddenly ambulant and thankful for a new lease on life, she wants to travel the world while she still can. "That's why I want to improve my English, to visit other countries," Flora confessed, "I don't know but maybe one day I cannot walk any more." She nodded earnestly, ending her soliloquy.

I was utterly blown away. Struggling to keep my composure, I joked that the self-professed shy talker had managed to go on for twice the time allowed. But Flora's story lingered in my head long after those haunting minutes. Her simple manners and understated appearance belied a bounty of inner strength. Life dealt her a tough hand of cards and she played it the best she could. There I was, sitting across from one of life's poker masters, grateful for a valuable lesson.

九龍的心結

Kowloon Complex

Kowloon is to Hong Kong as Brooklyn is to Manhattan.

The analogy is uncanny. Brooklyn is a reluctant sidekick to the much more glamorous Manhattan Island on the other side of the East River. Although Brooklyn is just one subway stop away from lower Manhattan, that two-minute train ride is what separates the men from the boys. Snooty Manhattanites, convinced that there is nothing in Brooklyn that you can't find back on the island, would never voluntarily cross the river unless some extraordinary reason warrants the inconvenience, such as to visit a friend who has thoughtlessly moved to the "boroughs." Brooklyn neighborhoods like Williamsburg and Brooklyn Heights are often touted by real estate agents using self-defeating sales pitches like "the city view on *this* side of the East River is so much better. Look how gorgeous Manhattan is!"

The sister rivalry between Brooklyn and Manhattan is a staple for New York-centric TV series like *Friends*, *Will & Grace* and *Sex and the City*. And the same rivalry exists between Kowloon and Hong Kong. If you still don't see the parallel, read the preceding paragraph again and replace "East River" with "Victoria Harbour," "Williamsburg" with "Whampoa" and "Brooklyn Heights" with "Olympic City" and you'll get my point. During the six years I spent in New York, I set foot in Brooklyn for all of three or four times, including twice for dinner at Peter Luger Steakhouse, one of the city's notorious tourist traps. My record of harbor-crossing to the Kowloon side is slightly better, averaging four or five times a year. I go there mostly for a concert at the Cultural Centre or an occasional singing gig at Harbour City.

But is Kowloon really Hong Kong's ugly stepsister? To the snooty Hong Konger, the Kowloon skyline is decidedly boring and never photographed. For the most part, the peninsula is unexcitingly flat, lacking the dramatic amphitheater-like topography on the Hong Kong side created by the contiguous ridgeline stretching from Mount Collinson (歌連臣山) on the east all the way to Lung Fu Shan (龍虎山) on the west. Kowloon is also devoid of any interesting architecture, unless you count the windowless, bathroom tiles-covered Cultural Centre and a planetarium that resembles a shiny bald head. Compared to their Hong Kong cousins, Kowloon folks are known to be somewhat rough around the edges in their manners, a prejudice my mom instilled in me when I was a boy.

For many years after Kowloon was ceded to Britain in the 1860s, European settlers used the rural peninsula only for recreational hunting while indigenous villagers worked their rice paddies and traded sandalwood. Kowloon remained largely undeveloped until the turn of the 20th Century when the Kowloon-Canton Railway (KCR) project began to urbanize the area. Still, land on the peninsula was rarely treated with care and respect. The original southern terminal of the KCR was built right in the middle of Tsim Sha Tsui, taking up valuable urban land and hindering long-term city planning. In the 1920s, a plot of reclaimed land near Kowloon Bay, originally slated for an upscale residential development, was purchased by the government to build an airfield. The site was later modified into the city's first international airport, limiting building heights across half of Kowloon and making the airport itself the world's most difficult one for landings and takeoffs. This urban anomaly was not corrected until 1998 when the government finally came to its senses and moved the airport to Lantau Island.

With a chip on their shoulders, Kowloonites keep a watchful eye on their sister island's every move and respond with the perfect countermove, creating an eerie parallel universe on the other side of the harbor. Shoppers' paradise Causeway Bay and its crown jewel Times Square meet their match with chaotic Mongkok and Langham Place. The 88-story skyscraper IFC Two is soon to be outdone by the 118-story ICC Tower that looks and sounds suspiciously similar to its rival. Middle-class micro-city Tai Koo Shing and up-market enclave Happy Valley lock horns with Mei Foo and Kowloon Tong. Every park, stadium and country club in Hong Kong has a counterpoint in Kowloon. Even the laid back afternoon tea at the Mandarin Oriental Hotel in Central cannot escape a challenge from the decidedly colonial Peninsula Hotel in Tsim Sha Tsui that offers its own 4 pm *prix-fixe*. Kowloonites do not take their sister rivalry lightly.

If *Sex and the City* were set in Hong Kong, you can bet Miranda Hobbes, ever the practical lawyer, would live in Kowloon and her posse would be doling out wise quips like "you know, *HK Magazine* says Kowloon is the new Hong Kong." And the cynical, self-deprecating red-head would roll her eyes and snap back, "whoever wrote *that* lives in Kowloon!" Touché, Ms. Hobbes.

Famous sight of a jumbo jet negotiating its way through residential buildings in the Kowloon Bay area

阿
家
與
禧
敏

Ah Gah and The Hill

I come from a big family. The age gap between the oldest and youngest siblings is well over a half generation. The five children, three boys and two girls, grew up in a crammed apartment in Tin Hau fighting over the bathroom and poking fun at each other every day. Born in the year of the tiger, my big sister Margaret combines the temperament of a ferocious feline and the maternal instincts of a loving tigress around her cubs. Ah Gah (阿家 Big Sis) – for that is how everyone in the family addresses her – was nothing short of a second mother to me. She would check my homework every night and buy me nifty school supplies as rewards for good grades.

When I turned four, Ah Gah got me a set of 24 coloring pencils in a sleek tin box. Printed on the box cover was the picture of a handsome sailing boat cutting through white waves on the open sea. Inside the box, the two-dozen sharp things were like a thousand Christmas gifts – the colors dazzled the eye and taught me words like "magenta" and "cobalt." I kept the pencils at the bottom of my drawer, where they remained largely unused. That was until I entered a coloring contest in kindergarten and won second prize. Over the years the tin box survived many moves, and is now tucked away somewhere in my parents' basement in Toronto.

Ah Gah and her little brother back in the days

Like everyone else in my family, Ah Gah has her quirks. Back in the days, we would hear her sing off-key to Whitney Houston's gut-wrenching ballads every morning while blasting away with the blow-dryer that turned her hair-do into a perpetual hair-don't. Then there was that small city of creams and lotions sprawling over her nightstand while a Shirley MacLaine paperback balanced precariously on the edge. If the former was the reason for her blinding facial glare each nightfall, then the latter would explain her propensity for drama and hair-trigger reactions to life's vicissitudes big and small.

Margaret now lives in Melbourne with her husband and daughter. Despite her geographical isolation from the rest of us, Ah Gah remains the glue that holds the rest of the family together. And after all these years, she is still the first person everyone calls upon whenever help is needed. Last year, when mom complained about her blood pressure, the ever-dutiful daughter spent nights researching online until she zeroed in on the perfect herbal remedy. And when her teenage daughter Hilary stressed over a school presentation, Margaret signed herself up for a public speaking workshop to make sure she was qualified to help. If anyone else had told me they did that, I would have laughed it off as a bad joke!

*　　*　　*

It is often said that the apple doesn't fall far from the tree. Surely enough, sixteen-year-old Hilary is blossoming into an upstanding young lady with a big heart. The Hill – for that is what I insist on calling my niece after the nickname was coined for Hillary Clinton during the 2008 presidential campaign – was struggling somewhat with her Grade 11 coursework and the looming threat of university entrance exams. Then Margaret remembered that I teach high school English and counsel students on college applications, and she sent me an email from Melbourne asking for my advice. I answered her distress call with great excitement, like Batman responding to the Bat Signal.

In the past weeks I have been calling the Hill to give her the lowdown on time management and study tactics – all the secrets and wisdom I accumulated through college and law school, and which I hold dear and near to my heart. And when the Hill told me she needed help with *Macbeth*, my heart skipped a beat. "Get your Skype account ready and fasten your seatbelt," I screamed into the telephone and proceeded to schedule one-on-one lessons via video-conference.

My eagerness to coach Hilary has little to do with my passion for teaching and much more to do with Margaret. Despite the many differences in our beliefs, values and not least our singing voices and opinions on hairstyles, Ah Gah was the guiding light in my formative years. All that faith, hope and love she poured into her baby brother have made him the man he is today. I have always wanted to do something for Margaret in return, but what does a forty-something middle-class suburban mother possibly need from me? It never occurred to me until now that helping her daughter is the best way to repay my big sister for everything she did for me. It is perhaps the *only* way.

* * *

The sheen has long vanished from the tin surface, brown rust advances. The writing on the cover peels away. But if Hilary is able to hold her own as she comes of age, I will give her the shabby box of coloring pencils and tell her what it means. And I will ask the Hill to pass it down like a prized family heirloom.

Laws of Nature

Back when I was still living in Toronto, my family and I used to spend a lot of time in front of the television set. If nothing good was on, we would flip to the Discovery Channel by default and watch ferocious felines rip apart an innocent zebra or a helpless gazelle. I often wondered why the camera crew would just stand on the sidelines and let the film roll, while savagery unfolded before their eyes. Would a successful rescue upset the order of the jungle and threaten the delicate balance of the entire ecosystem? Perhaps it is best not to interfere.

*　　*　　*

One afternoon I found myself shopping at City Super, a high-end grocery store in Hong Kong that sells mostly imported foods. At the cured meat counter I asked for 150 grams of *prosciutto* to make my own sandwich. While the meat boy was working the slicer, a pair of middle-aged women approached the counter.

City Super grocery store at the glitzy IFC Mall

"Check out these hams," the older of the two roused her companion in loud, accented Cantonese, pointing at the giant leg of *prosciutto di San Daniele* inside the glass cabinet. Her loudness drew my attention and her accent gave away her immigrant status. The younger of the two, perhaps a relative or a friend, picked up a sealed package of *jamón ibérico* from the nearby wicker basket and exclaimed, "$350 for so little meat? I am afraid to even touch it." But her promise was quickly broken, as she proceeded to bore her thumb into the prized meat before passing it to the older woman for further inspection.

"Is 156 okay, sir?" the meat boy asked me politely while reading the weight from the electronic scale. I nodded in the affirmative and dropped the purchase into my shopping cart. Watching me intently, the younger woman tapped her companion's arm in rapid succession. "Did you hear? $756 for that tiny amount!" she gasped, mistaking the ham's weight for its price and 156 for 756 (the numbers 1 and 7 are easily mixed up in Cantonese). Instead of correcting their misunderstanding, I gave the two women a friendly smile and disappeared into the eddies of shoppers.

I smiled at the two immigrants not because I found them amusing. I did so because in them I saw myself and my family many years ago. My family emigrated to Toronto in the 1980s as part of the Hong Kong Diaspora to escape the dreaded 1997 handover. Our move was marked by the same trials and tribulations experienced by many immigrant families: the struggle to blend in. But time and again we gave ourselves away with our cultural *faux pas*, some of them uncorrected for years. The two women's episode at City Super was a minor infraction compared to our social blunders too many and too embarrassing to enumerate.

Today, tens of thousands of new immigrants arrive in Hong Kong from Mainland China every year. Newcomers in pursuit of the Hong Kong Dream tend to be grass-roots families banished to immigrant ghettos like Tin Shui Wai (天水圍), euphemistically named "new towns" sprawling on the fringes of the city. A typical family comprises a father who makes minimum wage at a construction site or restaurant kitchen, a stay-at-home mother on a constant quest for part-time work, and young children struggling to fit in at school. Life is tough, but pervasive social prejudice makes it much tougher.

On average new immigrants spend more time watching local TV than the native Hong Konger. With little disposable income and a non-existent social life, they depend on free TV broadcasts as the only ready form of entertainment. Besides, primetime soap operas with convoluted plots of love, deceit and betrayal offer glimpses of Hong Kong society that may prove instructive in the new environment. It makes me wonder whether these reasons also explain my own family's TV addiction in Toronto back in the days.

*   *   *

I grabbed a baguette from the in-store bakery and pushed my shopping cart to the cash registers. In front of me, a man in his thirties conversed with his female companion in melodious Mandarin as he put down two bottles of mineral water and a $50 bill on the counter. Before I could figure out whether they were immigrants or tourists, the cashier girl, no more than sixteen years of age, rebuffed the Mainland Chinese customers in broken Mandarin, "you only pay for bread here!" Caught off guard, the man asked where he should be paying for his water instead. The teenager spoke again, this time louder and more annoyed than the last, "over there!" She pointed to the main registers on her right without looking up.

I removed the basket from my shopping cart and placed it on the counter and was immediately met with the same gruffness. "You too! You follow that man," the cashier barked. Noticing the disapproving frown between my eyebrows, she switched back to her mother tongue and apologized, "I'm sorry, do you speak Cantonese?" I nodded, struggling to understand what language had got to do with payment procedures. Somehow amused by the situation, the teenager let out a giggle, covering her mouth with one hand, and offered, "let me bag the baguette for you. But I'm sorry you still have to pay at the main registers. Please forgive the inconvenience, sir."

For a moment I was frozen, lost in my thoughts. In the capitalist jungle that is our city, even a sixteen-year-old has fangs. Should I have meddled during the cashier's assault on the Mainlander by reporting her behavior to the store manager and turned the predator into prey, the hunter into the hunted? The teenager could have received a reprimand or perhaps even lost her job. But in the end I did nothing. Like the Discovery Channel camera crew, I chose not to interfere with nature. It was nature of a different, more complex sort.

My Pet Peeves

We all have our pet peeves. They are the minor annoyances that make your skin crawl and your blood boil but you don't know why. The Cantonese expression *mo ming for hey* (無名火起), which literally means an "inexplicable fury," is a close cultural equivalent.

Pet peeves are by definition personal. What bothers you often doesn't get to the people around you, which makes them all the more frustrating. You are twice victimized when friends and family accuse you of being petty, uptight and unreasonable. The inexplicable fury can quickly turn into an uncontrollable wrath. Do you cringe when someone doesn't use a coaster, starts every sentence with the word "actually," presses his finger on your laptop screen, checks his Blackberry while talking to you or pushes the elevator's "close door" button in rapid succession when he sees you coming? How about a slow driver in a single-lane road, a chewing gum smacker on the train, a line cutter at the check-out counter or an open-mouth sneezer on a crowded bus? The list goes on and on.

Below is the "top ten" list of my personal pet peeves, obsessive-compulsively arranged in order of increasing annoyance.

1. Air Golf-swings – Golf is hardly a sport, at least according to the International Olympic Committee that year after year refuses to add it to the Olympic program. But in our topsy-turvy world, this lame pastime has become one of the most coveted social activities of our time. Self-proclaimed enthusiasts block pedestrian traffic with their clumsy club bags and pay a fortune just so they can walk on an oversized lawn. Still, nothing is more irritating than the stuck-up investment banker type who practices his swings with an imaginary golf-club in the elevator or taxi line and then checks to see if anyone is watching.

2. Unexpected Dinner Company – You have been looking forward to meeting up with an old friend for a night of stimulating conversation. Then *BAM*, he shows up with a total stranger, either a cousin visiting from California or a college roommate he has just run into in Wanchai ten minutes before seeing you. It would have been fine if your friend had asked for your consent beforehand and given you the opportunity to reschedule. A painfully awkward dinner ensues, and there won't be a next time.

3. The Lingering Waiter – At any given restaurant in Hong Kong, be it a Michelin-star winner at the Four Seasons or a hole-in-the-wall in old Sheung Wan, you finish your meal and the waiter dutifully brings the check, smiles, and then shocks you with the unthinkable: he announces the exact dollar amount of the bill and then stands there until you produce payment. You try to shoo him off in a subtle way but he stands his ground. After the waiter finally walks off with the credit card, your lady guest is compelled to thank you for the meal because she has just been told how much her birthday dinner cost, right down to the cents. "Did he pay the waiter to do that?" your guest wonders.

4. Out-of-control Children – Society has grown increasingly tolerant toward children. I am referring to those parents who take the notion of "boys will be boys" too far and let their kids run amuck in stores or restaurants terrorizing everyone around them. How you wish you had a hand grenade so that you could finish them off, parents and kids alike, in a single targeted blast! Then there are the obligatory crying babies on the long-haul flight from Hong Kong to New York. That's when you realize you have just spent a small fortune on a business class ticket for 16 hours of blood-curdling screams at 35,000 feet. No amount of ear-plugs, complaints to the cabin manager or dirty looks at the guilty parents can alter the reality: you are screwed. Moments of temporary reprieve from these pint-sized crying machines only give you a false sense of security, before they are back at it, louder than ever before, and knocking you right out of your seat.

5. "May I Help Choo" – This bizarre mispronunciation of the simple phrase "may I help you" can be heard across the service industry, uttered matter-of-factly by everyone from hotel managers to telephone operators. Originating in Hong Kong, the disturbing trend has shown signs of spreading across South East Asia to countries like Thailand and Indonesia that look to Hong Kong for best practices. Bad idea.

6. The Door Slammer – The basic courtesy of holding the door for the person behind you has yet to catch on in Asia. Every day I see heavy glass doors spring back and slam hard on the helpless mother pushing a baby stroller, the delivery man balancing a pile of packages and the octogenarian hunched over a walking cane. When you do hold the door for the needy, they will give you a surprised, grateful look and utter an almost tearful "thank you" in English. They know you are not from around here.

The last thing you want to see on a long-haul flight

7. The Zealous Churchgoer – We all have the right to worship. Organized religions are a wonderful thing until they are used as a credential or guarantee of character. We have all heard such nonsense as "I don't lie. I am a Christian," or "Linda will make a great manager. She goes to church every Sunday." Hypocrisy within the Asian church is the reason why both my brothers, still devout Baptists, have stopped attending the Sunday service altogether. Then there are the evangelicals who dispense unsolicited spiritual advice or pass moral judgment in the office or at a social dinner, shoving their beliefs down your throat and bringing the conversation to a screeching halt.

8. B.O. – Unlucky for me, my sharpest sense is my sense of smell. I have been cursed with an over-developed nose that allows me to pick up even the faintest odor like the proverbial canary in the mine. A whiff of body odor or bad breath is enough to turn my stomach and make me gag. As I struggle to breathe through my mouth, I wonder how aromatically challenged people can go through life without their loved ones ever telling them the truth. I also wonder why I wasn't born with an eagle's eye or a rabbit's ear instead – something a little more useful.

9. *The Loud Talker* – They are everywhere in Hong Kong and the cell phone is their weapon of choice. People talk on the phone at the top of their lungs in the elevator, at the restaurant, on the minibus and in a crowded movie theater. Privacy is clearly a low priority, as anyone within a 50-foot radius is let in on the most intimate details of their personal lives. It's a sonic invasion of personal space, a crime punishable by shoving their cell phones up their you-know-where.

10. *Racist Remarks* – Racism is largely condoned or even accepted in this part of the world, perhaps because of the unspoken pecking order among Asians which we so tacitly accept. The Japanese, being the wealthiest in the region, sit at the top of the food chain. After that come the Koreans and the ethnic Chinese, who rank above people of darker complexion from Thailand, the Philippines and Indonesia. Folks from the Indian subcontinent are at the bottom of the heap as a result of antiquated and vile racial stereotypes. In Hong Kong, South East Asian domestic helpers are frequent targets of racial jokes in the media and in social conversations. Children who act aggressively toward their foreign caretakers go unpunished, because the parents themselves are guilty of the very same offense.

*   *   *

I sometimes fantasize about being the King of the World, not the James Cameron at the 1998 Oscars kind but the Carrollean "off with his head" sort of all-powerful tyrant. I would hand down the death sentence to anyone who commits one of my pet peeves and watch them beg for mercy in front of a firing squad. And I would turn to my subjects and say, without batting an eyelid, "well, that should teach him a lesson." I guess that's just one of the many reasons why I am not king.

難
道
小
巴

總
是
黃
色
的

Why Must All Our Minibuses Be Yellow?

You hail it like a taxi but you share it shoulder-to-shoulder with strangers as you do a double-decker bus. Sixteen riders sit snugly in cellophane-wrapped seats, their eyes glued to the flickering speed display installed by law to discourage speeding. It is the omnipresent minibus: our perky, peculiar and indispensable means of public transport.

Invariably painted a soft hue of yellow, the minibus dons a green or red top (depending on its route) and sits on four dark-skinned tires with yellow rims that match the body. So long as the fare is paid, each passenger takes up a single seat and submits to the vagaries of the unpredictable driver. It is an egalitarian experience in an otherwise stratified society. Just when strangers start to bond and first acquaintanceships begin to blossom, one by one passengers holler their desired stops and return to their disparate lives.

A motorcade of minibuses queuing up for passengers

I take the green minibus to and from work every day. Passengers on my route tend to be ethnically diverse, from Caucasian expatriates and Southeast Asian domestic helpers to tourists from every corner of the world. Every now and then, an Indian or Pakistani rider surprises the cabin with his fluent Cantonese. As the LPG engine roars through the sinuous route, quiet passengers mind their own business while this pensive observer ponders over the living Benetton ad before him. One may easily mistake our city for the kind of multicultural utopia where different ethnic groups co-exist in perfect harmony and happy children of every color hold each other in warm embraces. Well, not quite.

America is called the "melting pot" because people of different ethnic backgrounds fuse into a singular society. Newcomers to the country shed their old identity and replace it with a new, I-am-an-American self-image in the name of "integration" and "assimilation." Woven of many different colored threads, the American tapestry invariably comes out red, white and blue. On the other hand, countries like Canada and Britain adopt a less coercive immigration policy called "multiculturalism." The model rejects the idea of a single, dominant social norm and demands its citizens accept and celebrate each other's distinct cultures. Multiculturalism is sometimes discredited for its tendency to let minorities sequester themselves from mainstream society, foster resentment from the majority and ultimately threaten the unity of a nation. The model nevertheless appears to be working fairly well for countries that have adopted it.

Hong Kong's policy toward its ethnic minorities is every bit as *laissez faire* as its economic philosophy. Enticed by a tax system so lenient the city was called a tax haven by the French President, foreigners flock to Hong Kong as a gateway to China without the travails of actually living *in* China. It is odd that a city as cosmopolitan as ours can get on without a set of coherent government policies toward its changing demographics. Our Equal Opportunities Commission is a bureaucratic mess, chaired by an elitist who was caught using the public coffers to pay for personal expenses. But even on the social level, interracial mingling is scant and superficial. Ethnic Chinese, comprising 95% of the population, prefer to stick to their own kind and keep the other 5% at a comfortable distance. We practice the Taoist creed of "see no evil, hear no evil," despite having *gweilo* (鬼佬, the historical derogation for Caucasian men) co-workers in the office and a *bun mui* (賓妹, a local slur for Filipino maids) at home. Foreigners, equally content to be left alone, share the city like quiet passengers on a minibus, anonymous and invisible. Like oil and water, the two simply don't mix.

One explanation for our social segregation is that reaching out to minorities takes time and patience. In our society of bottom lines and instant gratification, time is money and patience is as scarce as hen's teeth. Exhausted from a 12-hour day of mind-numbing work, few are in the mood for wishy-washy cultural exchange in a different language that ultimately doesn't benefit their wallets. Another explanation, more forgiving and less cynical than the first, is that few foreigners ever stay in Hong Kong long enough for relationships of any depth to take hold. Those who require a change of scenery will pack up and relocate to other equally exotic Asian cities like Singapore and Tokyo after a five-, six- year stint in Hong Kong. Others who have earned and saved enough can't wait to leave the maddening city and live out their retirement dream in a quaint little English town or their home village in the Philippines. People come and go through our revolving doors every day in much the same way passengers get on and off a minibus and never look back.

Caucasian expatriates in Hong Kong, unceremoniously referred to as "red beard and green eyes," live in a borrowed place on borrowed time. They commute between their Midlevels homes and Central skyscrapers during the week and clang bottles within their small circle of countrymen over the weekend, taking life one twelve-month lease at a time. Emotional investment in the city is carefully avoided and second-generation immigrants are unheard of. Things that are important to the expat community, such as the annual Rugby Sevens and Coldplay making a one-night stop, are irrelevant to a typical Hong Konger. But the *gweilo* can be equally blasé about local happenings. Talk-of-the-town topics like the Bus Uncle (巴士阿叔) saga and the death and resurrection of soap opera character Laughing Gor (Laughing 哥) somehow manage to fly completely under his radar screen. "Laughing who?" he asks.

There are reportedly 150,000 Filipinos living in Hong Kong. A vast majority of them work as domestic helpers, a trophy in every middle-class household. Despite living together in close quarters, self-important employers take no interest in the helpers' lives and minimize human interaction where possible. Words befitting household pets rather than employees, such as "lazy," "stupid" and "useless," swirl around in daily conversations. Children grow up thinking it's okay to mistreat others of a lesser perceived social status. Weeks ago, I witnessed a cranky minibus driver order two chatty Filipinas to move to the back of the bus because their Tagalog conversation was purportedly too "distracting" for safe driving. But the two Rosa Parks incarnates stood their ground and a 20-minute standoff ensued. The more defiant of the two snapped back, "I remember you – you never stop the bus when we ask you to. You treat our people very bad!"

A few months ago, Dil Bahadur Limbu, a 31-year-old park squatter of Nepalese descent, was shot and killed by a local policeman in a minor confrontation. Repeated warnings in Cantonese (a language Mr. Limbu had shown no signs of understanding) to no avail, the policeman shot the unarmed man twice, including once in the head. Law enforcement was quick to vouch for one of their own, offering callous explanations that further incensed the victim's family and the South Asian community. Perhaps the incident was simply a series of unfortunate events. Perhaps. But just the same, Mr. Limbu's needless death is an overdue wake-up call for the city to face up to a social problem that has so far been swept under the political rug. Concerted efforts to instill cultural sensitivity and encourage interracial understanding are a long time waiting. Perhaps every minibus should be repainted in rainbow colors as a reminder to all of us that yellow, after all, is no longer the only color around here.

灣仔的成長

A Little Bay No More

I visit my brother Kelvin and his family in Wanchai every once in a while. They live on the east end of Kennedy Road, an area that real estate brokers call "Midlevels East." Their apartment complex has an exit on Queen's Road East adjacent to the 63-story Hopewell Centre, once the tallest building in Hong Kong until the Bank of China Building snatched the title in 1989.

I follow each fraternal visit with a leisurely walk down Queen's Road East. The street is lined with a stretch of mom-and-pop stores selling picture frames and traditional rosewood furniture, and a couple of hole-in-the-wall juice vendors each with a half dozen electric blenders going at it at the same time. As I guzzle down my cantaloupe juice out on the sidewalk, I can't help but marvel at the little known fact that Queen's Road once marked the shoreline of Hong Kong Island. A century and a half ago, if you were to stand where I am standing, you would be smelling the briny sea breeze and watching fishing boat lights flicker against the moonlit silhouette of a barren Kowloon peninsula.

Queen's Road East at the turn of the century

But all that changed when the colonial government's massive reclamation projects, each one more ambitious than the last, began to extend the Wanchai area outward. Street by street, the island's shoreline edged northward, starting with Johnston Road where the tram tracks lie; followed by Hennessy Road, the main thoroughfare that connects Central to Causeway Bay; Lockhart Road, a mecca for lighting and bathroom fixtures; Jaffe Road, the closest thing to a red-light district on the Hong Kong side; Gloucester Road, an eight-lane freeway perennially blanketed with bumper-to-bumper traffic; and finally, the Harbour Road/ Convention Avenue twin backstreets that form the current shoreline of the island.

Wanchai is one of the oldest neighborhoods in Hong Kong. For many years after our city was ceded to the British in 1842, urban living was confined to the northwestern portion of island coast known to the locals as the "Four Rings." Right from the start, Central (literally, the middle ring) was handpicked by the early settlers to be the nerve center for all commercial and government activities. And when the Brits ran out of space in Central, action began to spill westward to Sheung Wan (the upper ring) and Sai Wan (the west ring) and eastward to Ha Wan (下環; the bottom ring). The settlers must have found the name "bottom ring" a bit unflattering, as the area was soon renamed Wanchai, which means, uh-hum, a little bay. Perhaps a more imposing name for the area was just not meant to be.

Today, Wanchai is a fast-growing and ever-changing city-within-a-city and offers a welcome alternative to tired old haunts like Lan Kwai Fong and SoHo. No longer content to simply mop up the leftover crowds from Central and Causeway Bay, Wanchai is pulling out all the stops to attract the bold and the beautiful, the young and the restless with new iconic hangouts such as The Pawn and the Star Street enclave. Brand new *avant-garde* apartment buildings like The Zenith and J Residence spring up every few months to lure yuppies away from Midlevels and Happy Valley. Whether Wanchai will finally succeed in reinventing itself and shaking off its second-tier image is still anyone's guess. As is the case for any up-and-coming new neighborhood, the Little Bay's fate now rests in the hands and wallets of the fickle, hard-to-please Friday night crowds.

Construction of Hopewell Centre II, a new development adjacent to the 28-year-old Hopewell Centre, is currently underway. The multi-billion project includes a five-star hotel, an upscale shopping center and highly coveted office space. Several months ago, the project developer announced that the original design would be significantly scaled down due to vehement opposition from local residents who expressed serious concerns over increased traffic, reduced greenery and blocked views. Among other concessions, the downscale will reduce the height of the hotel tower from the cloud-hugging 93 stories to a mere 55. The episode is more than just another David-versus-Goliath news story; it is evident that Wanchai now possesses the kind of social cohesion and civic power to influence major infrastructure projects. The area is well on its way to becoming an A-list neighborhood worthy of preservation and careful urban planning. It looks like our little bay is all grown up.

觀
點
與
角
度

A Matter of Taste

Warning: Generalizations ahead.

Chinese people are aesthetically challenged. So there I said it. There are exceptions of course. I.M. Pei gave the world the Louvre pyramid and recently the Museum of Islamic Art in Qatar. David Tang created fashion label Shanghai Tang and in the process popularized the concept of Chinese chic. Zhang Yimou (張藝謀), ever the worshipper of beauty, wowed us with the Beijing Olympics opening ceremony. And for every Pei, Tang and Zhang, there are thousands of other talented Chinese artists, architects and designers. But those outliers aside, the average Chinese person gets a failing grade in the subject of taste.

To commemorate Hong Kong's handover in 1997, the Chinese government bestowed upon its long-lost child the Golden Bauhinia sculpture, a massive gold-plated flower that sits on a granite pedestal shaped like the Great Wall. The road to hell is so often paved with good intentions. In this case, Beijing's show of generosity has left our city with a permanent eye-sore on the Wanchai waterfront. France gave America the Statue of Liberty and Japan lined Washington D.C.'s National Mall with breathtaking cherry blossoms. China gave us a tacky sculpture.

The gaudy Golden Bauhinia on the Wanchai waterfront

Ugly structures are everywhere in China and its territories, from the Oriental Pearl TV Tower in Shanghai to the Central Library Building in Hong Kong and the brand new Grand Lisboa in Macau, all brainchildren of local architects endorsed by numerous committees. It makes me cringe whenever I see on television how Chinese officials receive foreign dignitaries in one of those enormous meeting rooms with ugly, oversized armchairs and over-the-top flower arrangements featuring no less than 15 varieties of exotic flora, all against a Technicolor backdrop. "Less is more" is an axiom that has fallen on 1.3 billion pairs of deaf ears.

Decades of economic reforms in China have produced a generation of millionaires, but on that arduous road of social progress, good taste lags far behind wealth. That lag is most patently manifested in the stereotypical Mainland Chinese tourist covered with name brands from head to toe, wearing white socks with black Gucci loafers and shouting each other down outside the Chanel store in Tsim Sha Tsui. These familiar scenes remind me of the notorious Russian *nouveau riche* roaming the streets of London buying up half of Notting Hill. On the subject of fashion *faux pas*, before seas of Western tourists flooded Beijing during the 2008 Olympics, the city government distributed pamphlets to local residents dispensing fashion tips. "Citizens of Beijing, be sure not to wear more than three colors at a time!" When you need your government to tell you how to dress, you've got serious issues.

Then there is home decor. In any given Chinese home, convenience and budget always trump good taste. Nameless, pointless junk is shoved under, inside and above cheap furniture. The phenomenon transcends borders and socio-economic classes. Whether it is a low-income flat in the Shanghai outskirts, a middle-class condo in downtown Singapore or an exclusive duplex in Repulse Bay, if it is occupied by a Chinese household, expect to find clutter, clutter and more clutter. From the lonely brass-rimmed Seiko quartz clock pinned to the barren living room wall to the clunky 32-inch television set wedged inside a complicated oak-veneer IKEA cabinet and the chintzy chandelier hung way too high over an undersized dining table, every home is decidedly messy, clumsy and uncoordinated.

Bad taste is hardly the Chinese's privilege. Surely lapses in artistic judgment are not uncommon elsewhere in Asia. But for some reason the Japanese always seem to get it right, while Thai people are blessed with great interior design instincts and the Filipinos have their amazing musical gifts. So why are we such under-achievers in the department of taste? Perhaps our aesthetic flair was snuffed out by a decade of Cultural Revolution. Perhaps as a race we are conditioned to sacrifice style for more pressing priorities in life. Or perhaps *bon goût* is simply not in our genes. Whatever the explanation, I wonder whether we should accept defeat or keep holding our collective breath for a renaissance to jolt us out of our aesthetic coma.

Taste can neither be taught or bought. Either we are born with it or we acquire it by osmosis. The latter takes a porous mind and generations to take hold. Before we get there, however, we need to learn to be much less tolerant of ugliness and bad taste. That is the only place to start.

哦 和 一
她 個
的 早
上

An Aw-some Day

Back in my college days I went through an Amy Tan phase. I read everything the Chinese American writer had written, which was only three novels at the time but I enjoyed them just the same. So when a student approached me last week to help her with an assignment on *The Kitchen God's Wife*, Tan's most popular novel after *The Joy Luck Club*, I gladly took her on.

When I first met Lisa, she was everything I expected from an eleventh grader. She hated literature and hated talking about it even more. She dismissed *Kitchen* as "boring" and "pointless", although everything she knew about the novel was from *Cliff's Notes*. Having taught teenagers like Lisa for a number of years now, I have learned an obvious but often overlooked lesson: the most important part of teaching is getting the students to like what they do. It is also the most satisfying part.

Students being spoon-fed at a local secondary school

In our session this morning, Lisa and I picked out a few excerpts from *Kitchen* and together we discussed the writer's message underlying them. We explored the communication gaps between Pearl, the novel's protagonist, and her first-generation Chinese American mother. As we peeled through layers of subtext and went over the various themes, motifs and symbols, I began to notice a gradual transformation in my student's attitude – a transformation not unlike the one Pearl herself goes through in *Kitchen*. Halfway into our session, Lisa started to speak up and her posture went from a droopy slouch to almost a leap out of her chair. It was around that time that she uttered the "*aw*" word that lasted a good five seconds.

Aw (哦), a common Cantonese exclamation, carries a broad range of meanings. Depending on how long the sound is sustained and in what tone it is spoken, it can mean anything from "yeah, whatever…" to "OMG, I totally get it now!" I had no doubt that the *aw* I got from Lisa belonged to the second category. It is one of the most coveted responses a teacher can ever get, an indication that he is finally getting through to the student.

On my way to lunch after I finished with Lisa, I couldn't help but reflect on our education system. Lisa has the privilege of attending one of the handful of international schools in Hong Kong, and is therefore spared the woes of the local system where English is taught as a business tool instead of a language. But based on Lisa's initial reaction toward *Kitchen*, I am almost certain that her English teacher, Mr. Donovan, spends little to no time in class explaining why she and the rest of her class must endure the seeming torture of studying literature in the first place.

It wasn't Mr. Donovan's fault really. Teachers these days face unprecedented pressure from school administrators and parents to get through the basic curriculum under an impossible timetable. Any class time spent on things not directly related to preparing for public exams is deemed a distraction. How many complaints from angry parents does Mr. Donovan need to fend off before he realizes that it is in the best interest of his career to stick to doing old exams? This obsession with the bottom line has sucked the life out of our classrooms. Literature is one of its first victims.

I will see Lisa again in a week and we will go through more passages from Tan's novel. Unbeknownst to Lisa, her English tutor is on a one-man crusade in Hong Kong to help the next generation see literature for what it really is: a wonderful art form that is entertaining, inspiring and never for a moment, to use her own words, boring or pointless.

轎子的野史

The Dark History of Sedan Chairs

The annual Sedan Chair Race to raise money for charities and to promote Matilda Hospital （明德醫院） was held yesterday morning. Every November, teams representing their corporate sponsors, clad in over-the-top costumes and carrying equally over-the-top sedan chairs, loop around the three-quarter mile route along Mt. Kellett Road on the Peak.

I used to live right on the intersection where Mt. Kellett Road meets Homestead Road. As early as September each year, from my living room window I would see young men and women training for the event, a scene that became synonymous with the arrival of autumn. I watched the race last year with great interest and took a copious amount of pictures, though I was miffed that few local Chinese turned up for the event. This year I was all gung-ho about entering the race with people from work, only to find out that we missed the registration deadline by two weeks. In the end, I slept in that morning and wound up not watching the event altogether.

To make up for missing the hoopla, I decided to read up on how the whole idea of a sedan race came about in the first place. I have always been fascinated by the social history of Hong Kong, particularly the half-century period from 1898, when the New Territories was leased to the British, to the end of the Japanese occupation in 1945. Over the past few years, I have amassed a sizable collection of books on the city's historical streets and vanishing neighborhoods. With names like Arsenal, Ice House and Blue Pool, every street must have a storied past waiting to be discovered. Each time I flip through one of these books, I can't help but imagine what it would be like to stroll down a cobblestoned street at the turn of the century: women in their many-colored *qi pao* spreading laundry on droopy clotheslines outside their windows and street vendors hawking fresh chestnuts while red and green rickshaws swished merrily by.

The Peak Tram was introduced in 1888 by Governor Des Voeux to boost business for the ill-fated Peak Hotel near the modern-day Peak Galleria. Until then, the only way for Peak residents to commute between their prestigious residences at 1,800 feet and the bustling downtown area in Central was by sedan chairs. Local laborers on meager pay busted their backs carrying European *tai pan* up and down the torturous Old Peak Road, while their white passengers fluttered sandalwood fans and yawned at the verdant forest and gushing streams.

Matilda Hospital, located on Mt. Kellett Road, opened in 1907 to provide free medical care to expatriates. Scenes from the

Hollywood classic *Love is a Many-Splendored Thing* starring William Holden and Jennifer Jones (who wore funky eye make-up to make herself look "oriental") were filmed on location at the hospital. In the 1970s, the hospital faced financial ruin and the nurses came up with the idea of a sedan chair race to raise funds. Teams would race down Mt. Kellett Road following the same route as patients who were transported to the hospital after arriving by the Peak Tram.

Matilda Hospital on Mt. Kellett Road

I was recently at Matilda Hospital to visit a friend at the maternity ward. The facilities are top-notch and every patient enjoys a spectacular ocean view from their private room. I couldn't help but marvel at how good sick people had it back in those days. Staying there must not have been cheap, but getting in was the hardest part. For almost half a century, the Peak was off-limits to local Chinese. As a measure to prevent the spread of the Bubonic plague, the colonial government passed an ordinance in 1904 designating the Peak as an exclusive residential area reserved only for Europeans and government officials, effectively barring all Chinese citizens from entering the area. As if only the lowly Chinamen were capable of carrying the deadly disease!

The ordinance wasn't repealed until 1947, some 40 years after one of the most overtly racist pieces of legislation of our colonial history was inked. That means that six decades ago, if I were to tell my real estate broker that I wanted to rent the same apartment where I used to live, he probably would have tried to talk me out of it. "No, no, no, Mr. Ng," he would warn me in brusque Cantonese, "you see the Peak is *not* for people like you and me. Perhaps you would be more comfortable in Causeway Bay or Sheung Wan?" If America has its Montgomery bus, then Hong Kong has its sedan chairs. We sure have come a long way.

香港情懷

Hong Kong State of Mind

I

Once a month I spend a quiet evening in Wanchai. I will get a haircut, visit the big Chinese bookstore near Southorn Playground (修頓球場) and grab dinner from a neighborhood noodle house before heading home on a double-decker. The solitude is self-imposed and the private reverie cherished.

I had one of those evenings yesterday. I began the night at the hair salon, where a young apprentice named Durex gave me a wash followed by a pampering scalp massage befitting a world-class spa. I can never quite wrap my mind around why people here give themselves such bizarre names as "Concrete," "Jackal" and "Lazy," even though Lazy is a perfectly hardworking young lady who takes my order at Starbucks. With names like that, how can they ever expect to be taken seriously in life?

While my hairdresser snipped merrily away, I picked up the latest issue of *GQ (British Edition)* – one of my guilty pleasures – and started reading an article on the new Macau. I buried my head in the glossy pages while the young stylist dispensed unsolicited advice on male grooming and recommended drastic hair treatments. Sensing my mild annoyance, he changed the subject and asked if I was shopping for a new car, tipped off by the print ad for a new BMW model in the magazine I was reading. I forced a smile and said no.

I walked across the street to the multi-story Chinese bookstore that opens late into the night. The "local interests" section was on sale and I was happy to have spotted a new release on the history of Hong Kong during the Japanese occupation. It was a rare find, an exception rather than the rule. These days local bookstores in Hong Kong source over 80% of their stock from Taiwan. In our cash-rich, culture-poor city, fewer and fewer new titles get published every year. The perennial bestsellers are fortune-telling or *fengshui* manuals, investment how-to books and guidebooks to exotic foreign cities. Any tourist who stumbles into one of our local bookstores would easily conclude that we are a superstitious, money-grubbing bunch who can't wait to leave town the first chance we get. And he wouldn't be far off the mark.

I left the bookstore and walked through the wet markets reeking of fish. I found an empty table at my usual noodle house and ordered their signature fried *chow fun* with beef. The delicious, cooked-to-order Cantonese staple set me back all of HK$36.00 (around US$4.50). There were about two dozen other patrons in the restaurant lit by glaring white fluorescent tubes. Everyone there, regardless of gender, age and profession, glued their eyes to one of the four flat-screen televisions hung from the ceiling. A Cantonese soap opera was on, the usual plot line about feuding high-society families and conniving children caught in an inheritance battle. Television screens are a relatively recent addition to the local restaurant scene, but it has caught on like wildfire. It started two World Cups ago as a grass-roots movement by citizens who demanded access to soccer games anywhere, any time. The fixtures have remained long after the World Cup has ended. At any given restaurant in the city today, the only sounds you will hear are predictable melodrama dialogues drowned out by a sappy soundtrack. And if the televisions aren't turned on (during dim sum hours on weekends, for instance), you will find the husband reading the newspaper and the wife talking on the cell phone, while young children exercise their opposable thumbs on the PSP and the Filipino helper finishes every dish on the table. No one says a word to each other unless they want something. That must be human communication in its most sublime form.

I finished my meal and cleaned my teeth with a toothpick, a habit I took up since I moved here four years ago. It is a private activity on full public display, and the trick is to do it with utter nonchalance. Carrying a load of books, I decided to skip my usual night walk on Johnston Road and head straight to the bus stop. There, I found two high-school students whining about the cold weather. 15 degrees Celsius (60 Fahrenheit) and everyone bundles up as if it was the Russian winter. The teenage couple at the bus stop had just finished their days' work – seven hours of school plus another four hours of private tutoring – and began calculating how many marks they each needed on the biology exam to pull a B-average. Such is the state of our education system: students make their career choice at age 15 when they are streamed by subjects. Chemistry gets you into pharmacy, biology into medicine and economics into business. History, geography and Chinese literature are for losers. Classes are reduced to exam prep courses and teachers treated as oracles of public exam questions. Students are nothing but test-taking androids that memorize, regurgitate, and memorize some more. Few learn to reason and no one has an opinion.

A local noodle house in Wanchai

On my bus ride home, I took a seat in the last row of the upper deck, shoes off and head back. I gazed at the magnificent skyline before me. Only a handful of cities in the world rival Hong Kong as a true megalopolis: New York, London, Tokyo, Paris and Shanghai. To this biased citizen, Hong Kong is hands-down the most livable one among them. New York's infrastructure is shamefully antiquated; London is prohibitively expensive; Tokyo never stops treating you like a *gaijin* and Paris is as impenetrable as Tokyo except without the good manners. As for our old nemesis Shanghai, the city pampers and indulges until it doesn't. All hell breaks loose should anything happen and you find yourself at the mercy of the local, mostly corrupt, system. But however much I like Hong Kong, the city still comes out short on the intellectual front. Shallow, materialistic, culturally deprived and spiritually empty, each of these traits was borne out in some way by my evening in Wanchai. It only goes to show that no city is perfect.

II

It's that day of the month and once again I took the subway to Wanchai for a quiet, solitary evening. After I finished my haircut and dinner, I walked through the wet markets near Johnston Road to the nearby bus stop to catch a ride home. It was 10 o'clock at night and there were still people everywhere. Some were closing up for the night while others were devouring a late supper. A young couple flagged down a taxi, rushing to get home to catch the last bit of the nightly soap opera on television.

The No. 15 bus arrived in a few minutes. I took my usual seat in the last row of the double-decker's upper level, braving the air-conditioning at full blast. The bus was all but empty and I had the entire row to myself. As the roaring behemoth meandered up the hilly Stubbs Road, I took off my shoes, stretched my legs across three seats and drank in the spectacular city by night. The postcard-perfect view of Hong Kong always puts me in a reflective mood.

*   *   *

Hong Kong is a peculiar place. Seven million penny-smart, rough-around-the-edges denizens rub elbows with each other on a piece of land half the size of London. Joggers can cover the entire north shore of the main island in a couple of hours. Socially, there are no more than three or four degrees of separation among us. Five minutes into a conversation with a perfect stranger, you will find out his girlfriend Irene was in the same class as your brother-in-law at Berkeley. Irene, of course, now works in the same office building two floors down from you.

Controlled chaos on a busy Wanchai thoroughfare

I can be cynical about Hong Kong and for good reason. For starters, 90% of the population hasn't read a book since they left school – not unless you count tabloid magazines and their racy exposés on B-list local celebrities. As a result, citizens can't name the Vice President of the United States or the capital of Ireland to save their lives. If there were such a thing as an intellect index, it would hit just about rock bottom here. Then there is the boy cashier at McDonald's who wears a pair of Gucci sneakers and a Cartier watch that costs eight times his monthly salary. If there were such a thing as a materialism meter, it would be about at its peak.

Lounging at the back of the bus, I was once again overcome by an intense feeling of contentment. Despite the city's many flaws and foibles, there is nowhere else in the world where I feel so perfectly at ease. Hong Kong is the one place where things always have a wonderful way of working out for me, where I feel completely in my element. Every dream seems within reach if only I try hard enough to realize it. I can't help but wonder: is this what it feels like to be a white male in America?

The white American has it made. Everywhere he goes he is greeted by open doors. When you look like, sound like and act like the majority, you've got nothing to fear, nothing to prove. For those in the minority – and I have lived my entire adult life as a minority in North America – the onus is on *me* to prove that I am just as good as *them*. There is nothing racist about it, it is just a numbers game. Every Black, Asian or Hispanic American living alongside the white majority enters the race of life from a different starting point. That's the reason why I, like so many others, was inspired by Barack Obama when he became America's first minority president. All the odds he had to beat and all the naysayers he had to prove wrong to get to where he is today.

The notion of a different starting point is what makes Hong Kong a unique place for me. All my woes living in North America as a perennial outsider disappeared the moment I returned to Hong Kong. Here on my home turf, I can only be *better* than the majority, but never *worse*. For the first time in my adult life I know what it feels like to have the burden of proof go the other way. It is refreshing, empowering and intoxicating. According to comic book lore, when Superman first landed in that sleepy Kansas farm, he discovered not only that he was faster and stronger than everyone else, but that gravity on Earth was so weak he could fly like a speeding bullet. I don't feel like a super hero in Hong Kong, but I do feel just a bit more light-footed around here.

*   *   *

The double-decker dropped me off at my stop and billowed a puff of dark exhaust right in my face. The sooty fume was gradually replaced by a cool breeze that rustled through the nearby shrubs and brought with it the crisp smell of autumn. This city has a knack for making you love it and hate it at the same time. Do I love Hong Kong because I don't have to prove anything to anyone here? Or is it because there is something truly special and irresistible about the city? Whatever it is, I am forever thankful for my decision to move back here. Hong Kong is by no means perfect, but it is the place I call home.

我在三星期前死了

I Died Three Saturdays Ago

"I have never given much thought to how I would die," wrote Stephanie Meyer in the opening line of her bestselling vampire romance *Twilight*.

Well, neither have I. But on the ordinary summer morning of July 17, at a busy intersection on Pokfulam Road not 50 feet from my apartment building, my moment of reckoning finally arrived. And in the last few seconds of my life, I realized that death, that ultimate leveler of mankind, was not nearly as fearsome as I had thought. Nor was it as remote.

The section of Pokfulam Road near Hong Kong University

It is said that during the moments of death, your whole life would flash in front of your eyes. Not true. When the black Toyota minivan came out of nowhere and filled my dilating pupils with its ever-expanding windshield until metal and glass both faded into a whirlpool of nothingness, all I remembered seeing was those big brown eyes of the driver staring straight into my mortal soul. It is also said that in the final moments of life, regrets of all the things you never got to do would set in: the exotic places never visited, the millions never made, and the apology to an estranged brother never given. Not true again. Right when the vehicle knocked me out of consciousness, there were no memories of regret or penitence. The only thought I remembered having was my quiet acceptance: *so this is how it all ends*. And at that precise moment when my existence was snuffed out by the flick of a switch, I finally saw the beauty in death. The unspeakable beauty of finality and inevitability.

Until three weeks ago, the idea of dying, of life coming to an end, was the furthest thing from my mind. A few close calls here and there perhaps, like the time I ran a rental car into a fire hydrant after I first got my driver's license, or when I nearly drowned water-skiing without a life-jacket on Miami's South Beach. Then there was that rainy night two winters ago when I was in a taxi speeding down the Peak and the vehicle careened off the road and almost fell off the cliff. Other than those isolated incidents, I pretty much operated under the assumption that a few self-preserving measures – eating healthy, exercising regularly and not smoking – were all I needed to live to my eighties or nineties. But what do you know? It only took a freak accident to land me on page 7 of *The Apple Daily* (蘋果日報) the following day. *Jaywalker Killed on Pokfulam Road*, said the wistful headline in a modest font type. So much for trying to eat healthy.

Mortality is a reality that confounds us all, from the Ancient Greek philosopher and the Imperial Chinese emperor to anyone who has ever lost a family member to cancer or sat in front of the television watching stories of earthquakes or plane crashes. Even though death is all around us, few bother to give it much thought. When we are young and all we see are blue skies and cotton wool clouds lifted straight out of a storybook, we take risks that far exceed the rewards. Emboldened by the illusion of immortality, we run a yellow light in our souped up Honda or gobble down a nameless drink offered by a perfect stranger. As we get older, as that false sense of security begins to wane, we spend more time looking at the calendar than the watch. Anniversaries and birthdays are unwelcome reminders that life is but a race against time. The fear of mortality is what makes us take up the saxophone or buy a Porsche at age 45. Even so, to most people death remains something that doesn't really happen until it happens to them. Rarely in the human experience has a phenomenon so ubiquitous and constant been disregarded so completely.

As the saying goes, man proposes and God disposes. In my case it was as though God decided that my time on earth was not yet up, and He sent the reaper home empty-handed that morning. The driver managed to slam on the brakes just in time and I survived the impact completely unscathed. Nevertheless, the way I had pictured my death, those figments of my imagination, lingered long after that not-so-ordinary summer morning. The feeling of vulnerability from knowing that everything could have been taken away in a heartbeat creeps up on me every now and then. Sometimes when I see myself in the mirror, I can't help but wonder whether I am merely looking at the ghost of a person who died three Saturdays ago. Whenever these moribund thoughts pop into my head, the first few lines of John Keats' posthumous poem *On Death* – words that have taken on new meaning since the day I cheated death – will start ringing in my ears.

> *Can death be sleep, when life is but a dream,*
> *And scenes of bliss pass as a phantom by?*
> *The transient pleasures as a vision seem,*
> *And yet we think the greatest pain's to die.*

Part 2
The Things We Do

馬路上的大象

Pink Elephants On Our Streets

On any given day at any given time, from Kennedy Town to Chai Wan, Tuen Mun to Shatin, close your eyes and all you will hear are the roaring diesel engines of our double-decker buses. Hong Kong joins Britain, Russia, Singapore and Sri Lanka in the exclusive club of insane countries that still let these urban dinosaurs roam their streets. With its narrow roads, hilly topography and gridlocked traffic, Hong Kong is about the least qualified place on Earth to have two-story vehicles running around town. No matter which way you look at it, our double-deckers are out of place, out of scale and, at a time when carbon footprint is on everyone's lips, grossly out of style.

Public buses are the biggest polluters on our streets and they hit us on multiple fronts: air pollution, thermal pollution and noise pollution. We all know and mourn these familiar images: the double-decker lumbers off from the bus stop and billows a cloud of black smoke; pedestrians scramble to cover their mouths and turn their faces away, squinted eyes and furrowed brows. But whenever the thorny issue of air quality comes up, government officials conveniently point their fingers at Dongguan (東莞), a major industrial town in the Pearl River Delta and the smokestack of modern China, when the real culprit for our vanishing skyline is right here crawling in the city's veins. In fact, a majority of the double-deckers were purchased from England and Germany in the 1980s and 1990s and are way past their use-by date, kept on the road by bus companies reluctant to invest in newer, more fuel-efficient models. Recent government figures suggest that buses now account for as much as 40% of traffic emissions during rush hours.

During the steamy summer months from May through September, these old clunkers become heaters-on-wheels. Trapped by traffic lights, they form a wall of metal that blocks air flow and raises the outdoor temperature by several degrees. And because the massive vehicles need extra muscles to climb those hilly routes, they are fitted with much more powerful – and thus much noisier – engines than their European manufacturers have intended. I can almost picture those German engineers scratching their heads over the multi-million dollar orders faxed from Hong Kong and saying to their sales teams in mild disbelief, "okay, sure... if that's really what these suckers want."

But environmental travesties extend *inside* the bus. Air-conditioning in the cabin is always too cold, blasting arctic chills and burning even more diesel fuel. As any visitor to Hong Kong can attest, one of the curious sights in the city involves bus riders clad in sweaters and blazers in the middle of summer, still shivering in their seats while the blazing sun bears down on the rest of the city. But it gets worse. In the year 2000, bus companies began installing televisions on board – four screens on every bus – to make sure that even the airwaves are not spared from pollution. Riders hoping to find useful information on these screens, such as what the next stop is or where the bus is actually heading, are in for a big disappointment. Instead, they are bombarded with mind-numbing infomercials touting beauty products and hair loss treatments, an infernal torture that makes the telescreens in George Orwell's *1984* seem like a treat.

Then there are the safety concerns. Double-deckers, with their extra body weight and high center of gravity, are a menace on the road. Hungry for an adrenaline rush in Hong Kong? Forget the rollercoasters at Ocean Park and hop on a No. 23 bus that carves a hair-pin turn on the narrow overpass outside Canossa Hospital before it plunges down the precarious Garden Road. And if that doesn't do it for you, try No. 15 that swishes through the winding Peak Road, tilting slightly at each curve and screeching to a grinding halt whenever another double-decker approaches in the opposite lane before the two vehicles must maneuver around each other in slow motion. Even in less perilous circumstances, bus drivers have a knack for weaving between lanes as if they were driving Mini Coopers. Traffic accidents are a daily occurrence in Hong Kong, but those involving a double-decker are almost guaranteed to be sensational: a two-story bus flipping over a sharp turn like a fish lying on its side, riders being thrown out of the upper deck like human cannonballs, or the entire roof of the vehicle ripped off by a building protrusion like a convertible heading to the beach.

A common sight on the bus-infested streets of Hong Kong

We might have been willing to tolerate these oversized gas-guzzlers if the bus companies hadn't overwhelmed us with thousands of them. Kowloon Motor Bus (九巴), the leading bus operator in Hong Kong and one of the largest in the world, boasts a fleet of 4,000 buses on 400 routes, whereas New World (新巴) adds another 700 buses and 100 routes.

While bus companies in other countries are cutting routes as commuters opt for subways and trains, ours seem to be heading in the opposite direction. On Pokfulam Road where I live, a whopping 26 bus lines run on overlapping routes from the crack of dawn till the dead of night, each coming and going at 10-minute intervals. This leaves many of them virtually empty for most of the day outside the weekday rush hours and throws all claims of mass transit efficiency out the window.

At some point someone needs to ask the simple question: *why are there so many buses on our streets?* One possible explanation is that Hong Kongers are truly spoiled for convenience. Time-pressed citizens demand point-to-point bus services anywhere in the city – God forbid a commuter has to make a transfer – and hence the overlapping, intersecting bus routes. But I have lived in Hong Kong long enough to know that businesses won't do zilch for the public unless the economics justify it. A more plausible explanation is that a big chunk of the bus companies' revenue actually comes from advertising. With each side of the double-decker effectively a giant billboard, KMB and New World have every incentive to maximize advertising dollars by putting as many of them on the road as physically possible. So what if they block traffic and fill people's lungs with toxins? It is not as if our *laissez faire* government is about to stand up against corporatocrats in defense of public health and common sense.

Pink elephants are stampeding down our streets but no one is saying a word. Like so many other oddities in Hong Kong, the double-decker shenanigan is accepted here as a fact of life and even embraced for its colonial charm. Proposals to consolidate, rationalize and reduce bus routes have been tossed around for years but never materialized. Calls to replace old vehicles with diesel-electric hybrid models have fallen on deaf ears.

With the city's air quality deteriorating by the day, our patience and nostalgia for outdated technology are wearing thin. It's time we move on and get these God-forsaken things off the road. During the 1967 Riots, all bus services in the city were suspended and a new means of transport, the now ubiquitous minibus, sprang to life. If necessity is the mother of innovation, then let's send these outdated clunkers to the junkyard and hope that their absence will give way to a cleaner and quieter mode of mass transit and perhaps a better way of life.

To Eat or Not to Eat

That is the question.

Exotic animals and their body parts have always been an integral part of Chinese cuisine. They run the gamut from the pangolin (穿山甲) and the Himalayan palm civet (果子狸) to bear's paw and swallow's spit. In terms of universal appeal and indispensability, few things come close to the venerable shark's fin soup. The tradition of making soups using dorsal and pectoral fins from tiger sharks can be traced all the way back to the Ming imperial kitchen some 400 years ago. At any given Chinese restaurant in Hong Kong, whether it is a wedding banquet or a corporate function, a feast is not a feast without the obligatory soup served between the steamed grouper and the crispy chicken on a twelve-course menu. Omitting the soup, on the other hand, will not only disappoint and offend guests, but also stir up rumors of financial ruin shrouding the host for years to come. Contrary to common belief in the West, shark's fin soup is much more than a luxury. It is as much a part of the Cantonese culture as it is a social statement. It is our way of life.

The debate over the ecological impact and political correctness of eating shark's fin first gained traction with the international press in the early 2000s. In the years since, with mounting pressure from environmentalist groups to protect other endangered sea creatures like the blue-fin tuna and the Siberian sturgeon, the question of whether restaurants should continue serving our favorite soup has taken on new urgency. The whole debate got under my skin because, on a selfish level, I genuinely enjoy the soup. Those precious shreds of cartilage floating in a delicious golden brown broth always bring back fond childhood memories of accompanying my parents to a glamorous Chinese banquet lifted straight from a Zhang Yimou (張藝謀) movie set. On a more altruistic level, I was miffed because a slice of our cultural heritage is under siege. Once again, the Chinese ingenuity that turns the most improbable of ingredients into *haute cuisine* is being vilified as third-world savagery. It made me want to order the soup even more just as an act of defiance against Western prejudices.

That was until the ghastly reality of finning hit me like a ton of bricks, shattering all romanticism and sentimentality surrounding our culinary tradition. Look up the phrase "shark finning" on YouTube and you will find hundreds of graphic videos of fishermen hacking the fins off live sharks before the finless things are unceremoniously tossed back into the bloodied ocean to die a slow death. You would think humanity has made enough progress not to tolerate such cruelty even to animals. It makes me wonder why finning remains legal in most international waters when equally condemnable acts like tusking elephants and beheading gorillas are banned under conservation laws. After the gruesome rite of slicing and chopping, heaps of harvested fins are then fork-lifted from the trawler and taken to markets by the truckload, fetching as much as US$500 per kilogram. That's enough financial incentive for fishermen in impoverished Latin America and Africa to switch from fishing to much more lucrative finning. But because only 30 out of 440 species of sharks have fins that are suitable for soups and most rookie finners can't tell one species from another, thousands of unsold fins are left to rot in fish markets all over Asia.

Shark finning is a sight that is far from appetizing

Inhumanity is one thing, endangerment or even extinction is quite another. The phenomenal growth in China's middle class has fueled the exploding demand for shark's fin, both for gastronomic pleasure and as a status symbol. And whenever the Mainland Chinese start to like something, they go at it like there's no tomorrow. That, together with the insatiable appetite for fins in Hong Kong where nearly 80% of the world's fin trade is handled, has created a recipe for the undoing of soup-worthy species like the tiger, the sandbar and the hammerhead. According to studies by animal welfare watchdogs, as many as 100 million sharks are killed every year for their fins and some species have declined by over 90% in the past two to three decades, a period that coincides with China's economic ascent. Considering that some sharks, such as the lemon and the spurdog, take up to 20 years to mature and produce very few young, it is not surprising that 64 species of oceanic sharks have now been placed on the "Red List" by the International Union for Conservation of Nature (IUCN), a leading conservationist group.

Cruelty and endangerment are the two principal arguments against shark finning. But so much of the first argument turns on our personal philosophy of our relationship with mother nature. Who is to say, for instance, that slaughtering an innocent cow, with tears welling in its eyes, is any less cruel? As for the second argument, even scholars and scientists disagree on the causal link between finning and the decline in shark populations and whether the threat of extinction has been grossly overstated. In the end, the decision to eat or not to eat comes down to one simple analysis: the proportionality test. What do we stand to lose by taking shark's fin soup off the restaurant menu to discourage finning? After all, soup eaters know all too well that the fins themselves have no taste – all the wonderful aroma and flavors come from the chicken and dried ham in the broth. To keep our age-old tradition alive, restaurant chefs can easily substitute shark's fin with another ingredient of a similar texture and color, and their soup will taste every bit as good. We have endured other small inconveniences in life before, haven't we? Many years ago we sacrificed some of our cachet and tradition by saying no to ivory and fur. We gave up that bone-colored ornament at home and got by without the hairy coat in the closet. No skin off our back. But for those species we trap and kill, it is a matter of survival and extinction. The proportional impact on humans versus animals is as clear as day.

Because fishing bans are notoriously hard to enforce, we the consumers alone can reverse the ecological degradation by cutting the overpriced soup from our diet and drying up the global demand for fins. And if after all that you are still unconvinced, consider this: how much mercury and other toxins must have accumulated in the body of an adult shark, nature's most formidable predator at the top of the food chain, by the time it is finned and put on your dinner table? Bon appétit.

What's in a Cup

I

People who have just moved to America enjoy ranting about their cultural shock in the Land of the Free: the rude U.S. customs officers, the broken health care system and the way families load up on junk food and frozen dinners at the grocery store every weekend. But few subjects stir greater emotion than the God-awful American coffee.

For a country that puts a Starbucks in every corner of the world and where the Morning Joe verges on a national addiction, America seems decidedly incapable of brewing a decent cup of coffee. Back in my high school days in Europe, I used to take a shot of espresso after every meal and guzzle down many more cups while hanging out with equally nocturnal friends in my dorm room late into the night. The habit came to a grinding (pun intended) halt when I moved to Philadelphia for college. I remember the rude awakening when I got my first steamy order the day I arrived on campus. Offended by the flimsy paper cup and shocked by the utter tastelessness of its content, I kept adding more sugar and "half-and-half" in hopes of reviving the brown water. But it was no use, and I switched to drinking tea shortly thereafter.

So what's wrong with coffee in America? Everyone has a different theory and even experts disagree. I believe it all boils (pun intended) down to two things: preparation and serving. Instead of using the simple yet effective moka pot or *cafetière* the way they do in Italy and France, Americans invented the electric drip brewer. The machine works by letting hot water drip on ground coffee beans held in a paper filter before the droplets collect in a glass flask kept warm by a hot plate. You have to wonder: how can anything taste good after seeping through a piece of soaked paper?

On the issue of serving coffee, America's obsession with paper continues. The practice is driven by the nation's insistence on having everything "on-the-go." Therein lies the fundamental difference between the coffee culture in America and in Europe. Coffee in Europe is something to savor with friends and family after a hearty meal or over a leisurely conversation. By contrast, Americans drink coffee largely for the caffeine kick. The beverage has been reduced to a mere chemical stimulant to shock the system before a hard day's work. And this is where the paper cup comes in: to make it possible for the time-pressed working Joe to gulp down his go-juice in the car, on the subway or at the morning meeting. From McDonald's and Dunkin Donuts to the quaint little al fresco café in small town U.S.A., the paper cup has replaced white crockery and makes the already poorly prepared coffee even harder to swallow, both literally and figuratively.

Serving coffee in paper cups is not only a major *faux pas* in France and Italy punishable by public condemnation, it is also environmentally unfriendly. I for one find the practice no less absurd than drinking beer with a straw or sipping red wine from a Styrofoam cup. In fact, every physicality of a beverage container, from its shape and texture to its temperature and conductivity affects the drinker's overall experience. Any Chinese tea *aficionado* would tell you that the tea cup itself matters just as much as the quality of the tea leaves.

Two weeks ago I succumbed to Nespresso's aggressive marketing campaign and bought myself one of their sleek coffee makers after trying it out at the store. The machine brews a rich, authentic cup of espresso and cappuccino and is aesthetically pleasing. In keeping with the design trend started by Bang & Olufsen and KitchenAid, household appliances these days are as much a fashion statement as they are functional, rising to furniture status and coming out of the shadowy corners of the kitchen into the living room. Perched handsomely on my mini-bar counter, the little red cube instantly turns my dining room into a personal coffee shop and fills the space with the irresistible aroma of *grand cru* coffee beans. And so after my long hiatus from drinking coffee every day, I have officially fallen off the wagon. It feels just like reuniting with a long-lost friend.

II

My earliest memory of coffee was my father's large ceramic cup with Chinese inscriptions, an unlikely choice for a coffee mug. Before he retired a decade ago, my Dad was a freelance illustrator for a handful of local newspapers in Hong Kong. For four decades, he worked his paintbrushes and black ink every day at home in his snug corner, stealing noisy slurps from his signature coffee cup buried somewhere on his perennially cluttered desk. Every day I would hear the familiar noise of the rattling teaspoon as he stirred granulated instant coffee with powdered creamer and condensed milk. This explained why growing up we always had a sticky jar of yellowish curd in the fridge.

It wasn't until many years later that I found out instant coffee was something coffee drinkers scoff at because the powder is made from the lowest quality beans. Indeed, instant coffee has lost much of its popularity in Hong Kong since my early childhood. These days discerning consumers demand authenticity and opt for a fresh brew. Unwilling to sacrifice precious countertop space in their kitchen for a bulky coffee machine, drinkers have all but given up preparing their own coffee at home. It also seems far more debonair to walk into a Starbucks and walk out with a decaf double venti non-fat latte macchiato. All of that has sealed the fate of the decidedly unsophisticated instant coffee.

No discussion of Hong Kong's coffee-drinking culture is complete without mentioning the *cha chaan teng* (茶餐廳) phenomenon. They are local café-restaurants that offer an impossible variety of local and Western food and beverages perfected to satisfy our peculiar palate. From French toast and spaghetti Bolognese to beef curry and Cantonese fried rice, each dish is served on pastel-colored plastic plates straight out of an Easy-Bake Oven toy set.

Cha chaan teng is best known for its rather curious, some think off-putting, way of preparing English tea by squeezing the beverage out of tea leaves held in a nylon net resembling a woman's pantyhose, and hence the gimmicky handle "stocking milk tea." *Yuanyang* (鴛鴦), which literally means a mandarin duck couple, is another popular local concoction. Served either hot or iced, the beverage boasts the forbidding formula of mixing freshly brewed coffee with English tea. That's right, the same

English tea that drips out of those soaked nylon nets! Whether or not it is your cup of tea (pun intended), *yuanyang* is a Hong Kong invention that epitomizes the eclectic blend of old colonial elements and Chinese sensibilities that so essentially defines our city.

A cha chaan teng barman preparing a pot of milk tea

Our continued search for a cultural identity and increasing awareness of heritage protection have brought renewed interest in the *cha chaan teng* culture. There are even talks to enter this bit of the city's unique culture to UNESCO's biennial list of *Masterpieces of the Oral and Intangible Heritage of Humanity*, to be honored alongside Georgia's polyphonic singing and Japan's *noh* theater. In the 1990s, Tsui Wah Restaurant Group (翠華餐廳) breathed new life into the fragmented *cha chaan teng* market with a novel business model: a café-restaurant chain. Today, Tsui Wah operates over a dozen restaurants all over the city, several of which open 24 hours a day, becoming a *de facto* cafeteria for taxi-drivers, teenage coteries, drunken bar rats and other city nocturnals. With its extensive menu and no-nonsense staff, Tsui Wah has carved a niche for itself and managed to survive the onslaught of foreign café chains and competition from traditional restaurants. Its success story is a testament to the business savvy for which Hong Kong Chinese are known throughout Asia.

So how does a cup of coffee from a *cha chaan teng* measure up? In Hong Kong, the quality of any hot beverage is judged by, above all other measures, the quality of *heung wat* (香滑; aroma and smoothness). To achieve this easily achievable goal, a generous amount of evaporated milk is used to create a sort of *café au lait* with a local twist. It just so happens that this particular coffee critic is not a big fan of any milk-based drink due in part to his lactose intolerance. And so he must regretfully give Hong Kong's creamy coffee the thumbs-down, while expecting impassioned disagreement from the drink's many loyal devotees, including, above all, his own father who to this date still clings to the vanishing practice of using condensed milk to sweeten his caffeine kick.

理性的日全蝕 **Total Eclipse of the Mind**

The local news report last night covered the solar eclipse that has captured the imagination of millions in China and India. The news report ended with snippets on the annual Hong Kong Book Fair and an update on the drawn-out courtroom battle over the family fortune of Nina Wang (龔如心), the late chairlady of the Chinachem Group and the richest woman in Asia at the time of her death. The three news stories left me with a curious question: what do they all have in common? Then it dawned on me that each of the stories, unrelated as they may seem, provides a window on how superstition still figures prominently in our everyday life. A decade into the new millennium, some 200 years after the birth of Charles Darwin and four decades since Apollo 11 landed on the moon, folk beliefs and practices have shown no signs of backing down here in Hong Kong.

Nina Wang, the late heiress to the Chinachem empire

We begin with the fascinating tale of the pigtailed billionaire Nina Wang. Devastated by the disappearance of her husband, believed to have been killed by kidnappers, Mrs. Wang spent her life building a real estate empire while teetering on the brink of a mental breakdown. In life, the widow succumbed to the persuasion of amateur *fengshui* master and self-proclaimed kept man Tony Chan (陳振聰). In death, she is the protagonist of a sensational courtroom drama that pits the consummate gold-digger against the Wang family and their charitable foundation. Legal battles over family fortunes are hardly a novel concept in Hong Kong – just look at the Hotungs and the Kwok brothers.

What's shocking about the Nina Wang saga are the blow-by-blow details of the bizarre and often disturbing superstitious rituals performed by the widow in hope of bringing back a dead husband. From burying amulets in "*fengshui* holes" dug all over the city to torching wads of cold cash in the dead of night, the mind-boggling rituals border on witchcraft and provide rich fodder for daily water-cooler conversations across the city.

Superstition is a universal human trait. In the West, university students wear their lucky underwear to final exams and old ladies toss spilled salt over their left shoulder to ward off bad luck. Professional athletes in America are notorious for their sports superstitions and swear by practices like spitting into one's hands before picking up a baseball bat or never washing a basketball jersey despite obvious repercussions. In Asia, where folklore, tradition and religion merge into one, superstitious beliefs are part of a social code to be followed out of both self-interest and consideration for others. Hong Kong, ever the quirky one, takes it one step further and elevates folk beliefs to an academic discipline studied by citizens across age groups and socio-economic classes. *Fengshui* advisors, fortune-tellers and *suen mang si* (算命師; literally, life calculation masters) command celebrity status and charge exorbitant sums for unverifiable and therefore irrefutable advice. In the case of Tony Chan, his No. 1 client reportedly paid him HK$700 million in cash delivered to his apartment in a cargo truck.

At this year's Hong Kong Book Fair, opened just yesterday at the Convention Centre in Wanchai, the bestseller list reflects the current economic mood. Publishers find readers in a recession shifting away from get-rich-fast investors' guides, the perennial favorites during the bull market, to fortune-telling manuals. It is not difficult to understand why. For a city where pragmatism is the only religion, these manuals not only let us in on what the future holds but also teach us how to change it for the better, such as by seeking out relatives and friends identified as *gwai-yen* (貴人; people who bring luck) and avoiding numbers incompatible with one's astrology.

Superstition is often a barometer of confidence in ourselves and our society. Whether it is taking a public exam, starting a new business, finding the love of your life or something as mundane as taking a bus to work, everything we do is affected by a confluence of countless variables and beset by risks and uncertainties. And when the search for reassurance and answers turns desperate, superstition answers the call and in the process becomes an integral part of our collective psyche. Even though on a rational level we know that these beliefs fly in the face of everything our modern education has taught us, on a practical level we want to hedge our bets on the off-chance that there is more to life than a series of random events. That is precisely why some of us continue to pay serious money for license plates filled with the lucky numbers 3 and 8, why we would be hard-pressed to find a 4th, 13th, 14th or 24th floor in any high-rise building, and why we decide to butcher our language by calling an empty box a "fortune box," just because the Cantonese word for "empty" (空) happens to be a homophone for "misfortune" (凶).

The longest total solar eclipse in centuries packed the streets of Tongling (銅陵), a tiny mountain city in China's Anhui (安徽) province, with sun-chasers eager to behold one of nature's awesome spectacles. It wasn't that long ago when people in China still believed that solar eclipses were a result of the celestial dog gobbling up the sun. Even in this day and age, many in India still view the astronomical phenomenon with unease and trepidation. The eclipse sent thousands across India running to holy rivers for a ritual bath to ward off evil spirits. Here in Hong Kong, we scoff at these backward behaviors, but few bother to reflect on our own belief system and realize that the bathers are no sillier than those among us who forbid a pregnant woman from attending a funeral or wear one of those ugly citrine wrist bracelets to attract wealth and fortune. We are all just hedging our bets.

保身祕訣

The Secrets of Self-Preservation

I have had this stubborn, persistent dry cough for about a month now. Multiple visits to the doctor's office have been paid and a cocktail of anti-allergic drugs, cough syrup and inhaled steroid has been prescribed to little avail. Cold drinks and sugary food tend to irritate my windpipe and I have summarily cut them from my diet. But one irritant remains as unavoidable as April showers: the sooty air from rush hour traffic in Central.

It was a *déjà vu* of what happened three years ago when I first moved to Hong Kong. The dry cough was just one of the host of health issues that beset the early months of my repatriation. There were also the blood-shot eyes, the throbbing migraine and even a curious case of impaired short-term memory, all seemingly attributable to the poor air quality here. War stories like mine echo across the expatriate community and survey after survey has cited Hong Kong's notorious pollution problem as the singular reason for talents to opt for better homesteads in Singapore and Tokyo.

In a city where long working hours, skipped meals and five-hour sleeps are the rule rather than the exception, health often takes a backseat to life's other priorities and demands. To many, exercise means the annual hike to their grandparents' grave sites as part of the *Ching Ming* (清明; tomb sweeping festival) tradition. Perhaps the city itself is to share the blame for its citizens' aversion to exercise. There is far too much traffic and too many hills for leisurely cycling or jogging. Cyclists and joggers take to the streets at the risk of filling their lungs with toxic pollutants or being run over by a twelve-ton double-decker bus. You can't avoid these urban perils unless you live somewhere along the privileged residential belt that loops counter-clockwise from Bowen Road through the Midlevels and Pokfulam to the sandy beaches along the south coast, ending with low-density Tai Tam and Jardine's Lookout on the east side of the island. But if you don't feel like burning half of your paycheck on rent, then the gym becomes your only source of risk-free exercise. But the gym culture has yet to take hold among the local population. Most gym rats on the treadmill or in the weight room are foreigners, and the few locals who sweat it out at the gym are invariably branded by family and friends as leading some sort of alternative, health-obsessed lifestyle.

But where we lack in exercising, we make up for by the meticulous care we take to monitor our daily diet. If the stereotypical American has no qualms about washing down burgers and French fries with a pint of beer, and Europeans are far too willing to indulge in excessive wine and tobacco, then Hong Kongers genuinely treat their bodies as their temples, imposing strict quotas on some foods and avoiding others altogether. According to conventional wisdom, certain common foods like duck and shellfish are considered "toxic" and should be consumed in moderate amounts. Children learn to control their intake of toxic fruits like lychee, pineapple and mango before they learn their alphabet. What's more, cold drinks of any kind are universally condemned as harmful to your system, which explains why restaurants serve their customers warm water even on the hottest of summer days.

Lychees, one of the most toxic foods according to Chinese lore

Then there is the concept of *yit hey* (熱氣). Largely undocumented in Western medicine, it is one of the key tenets of Chinese medicine and is followed by Hong Kongers with utmost deference, myself included. *Yit hey* is an adjective that describes a blacklist of foods rife with "hot energy" which will wreak havoc in the body if consumed in excess, causing bad skin, sore throats, oral ulcers or all of the above. The list covers anything that is deep fried, roasted, grilled and spicy, ranging from guilty pleasures like potato chips and chocolates to seemingly innocuous staples like coffee and cookies. The adjective can also be used to describe a person who has too much of this hot energy, typically someone of weak dietary discipline who consumes more blacklisted items than his body can handle. To restore his *yin-yang* balance, he must take copious amounts of herbal medicine, failing which the only sure remedy is the homemade soup.

No one is more devoted to the practice of *bo sun* (補身; literally, preservation of the body) than the Cantonese, and few things are more revered than mom's trusty homemade soups. This traditional form of detoxification promises to reboot the system and uses the most improbable of ingredients. From silkworms and sea-horses to deer genitals and pig brains, nothing is off limits and everything is fair game. Each ingredient going into the soup is picked for a specific medical efficacy. On any given night, dutiful mothers-*cum*-alchemists follow their secret family recipes and serve up bowls of steamy potion to eagerly awaiting family members. Smokers, drinkers, night owls and others with unhealthy habits guzzle down these time-tested elixirs and atone for every sin committed against the body.

I haven't lived with my mom since I left home for boarding school in my teens. That means I haven't had the privilege of her nightly homemade soups for just as long. I am certain that my dry cough would have gone away much earlier had she been around to work her magic on me. Instead, I suck my steroid inhaler twice a day and still find myself coughing my lungs out and having to dodge death stares from hypochondriacs in the elevator. After each fit of coughing, I mentally go through everything I have eaten that day hoping to pinpoint the culprit responsible for my condition, a habit that reminds me of how firmly these diet-based health beliefs are ingrained in our psyche. Under our belief system, oral remedies and dietary abstinence are paramount, whereas exercise and clean air, as fundamental as they are to a healthy lifestyle in the West, are deemed secondary. Then again, with obesity and heart diseases approaching a national crisis in the United States, Americans should take a hard look at their diet and borrow a page from our self-preservation playbook. When it comes to the issue of health, it seems we all have something to learn from each other.

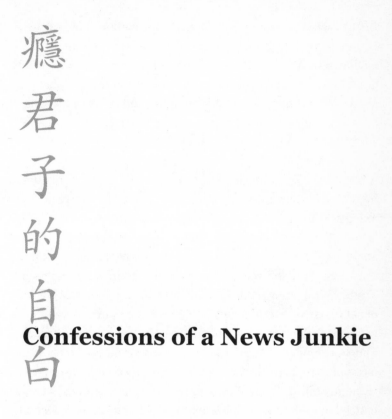

瘾
君
子
的
自
白

Confessions of a News Junkie

I

I am addicted to news.

Everyday I devour *The International Herald Tribune* more enthusiastically than I do my lunch. At the gym I work out to *60 Minutes* and CBC's *World At Six* instead of the Black Eyed Peas or Beyoncé. After a day's work, I risk motion sickness on the mini-bus to watch Katie Couric and Brian Williams at their anchor desks on my 3.5 inch iPhone screen. And when I finally get home,

I change out of my work clothes in front of the television playing pre-recorded evening news on TVB, a local television channel.

In this age of constant and instant information flow, idleness is a punishment no one deserves. Nothing irks me more than having to twiddle my thumbs on the subway train or stare at the dandruffed hair of the man standing in front of me in a restaurant queue. With a newspaper or iPhone in hand, I turn every wait, long and short, into precious moments of mental stimulation while staying on top of world events.

A person's news source is like his shoes – it tells you a lot about him. Casual questions like "what magazines do you read?" or "what's your favorite newspaper?" can uncover interesting information about the respondent or even change your opinion about him, for better or for worse. Some people never follow the news and don't seem to be bothered by it, while others lie about their reading habit to impress or to save face. During one of her disastrous interviews with CBS's Katie Couric, Sarah Palin was asked what newspapers and magazines she reads regularly. Caught completely off-guard by an otherwise fair and innocuous question, the then-Alaska governor and VP candidate stuttered, "Emmm... all of them." Katie gave her signature head tilt and batted her eyelids in complete disbelief. After losing the election, the incredibly well-read governor told reporters that she might run for president in 2012. Good luck debating Obama, Sarah.

Because the choice of news source is so personal and revealing, it often sparks lively if not heated debates among friends and family. Last month I spent an entire night with my brother Kelvin discussing our favorite magazines. I have been an avid reader and subscriber of *The Economist* for sixteen years. During our conversation, I confessed to Kelvin that, my long-term relationship with the magazine notwithstanding, I let my subscription lapse several months ago because the love is simply gone. In recent years I am increasingly finding their writing wishy-washy and their articles heavy on facts but light on analysis. But my sentiment aside, *The Economist* is still by far the best weekly news magazine in print.

Some of the popular news magazines on the market

Kelvin has a subscription to *Time* magazine, an American publication which I genuinely dislike. The problem with *Time* is not so much its writing but its coverage. Like everything else in the American pop culture, *Time* is consumer-driven and is too willing to pander to a public that demands instant gratification, resulting in a magazine that lacks imagination and character. A typical weekly issue comprises a cover story on the *sujet de la semaine* (invariably about the wars in Iraq and Afghanistan or the battered economy), two pages on the salmonella outbreak and five reasons why the nation needs renewable energy. It is television news on paper, but in many more words.

These days, whenever I pick up the newspaper or listen to my podcast, all I get is bad news. On *60 Minutes* this week, seasoned journalist Scott Pelley reported on the closing of DHL's operations in Wilmington, Ohio, instantly putting thousands of families out of work. A tearful mother said she was forced to pull her son out of college because she could no longer afford his tuition. Just last week, a drunk driver in Hong Kong swerved his truck into oncoming traffic, killing five passengers and the driver of a taxi. Distraught families rushed to the scene and pleaded with the Chief Executive to tighten drunk-driving legislation. These stories tug at our heartstrings and at the same time make me wonder about the kinds of things I have been writing about in my column. All that raving and ranting about Hong Kong's minor imperfections, the staple for my articles, becomes suddenly irrelevant in the face of job losses and tragic deaths. But how long are we supposed to wallow in despondency and at what point do we snap out of it and get on with our lives? I don't know the answers to these questions. Until I figure it out, I will stick to writing about the things I want to write about.

II

Lifestyle magazines often feature a section where celebrities make a list of the ten things they can't live without. Brad Pitt goes everywhere with his Ray-Ban aviator sunglasses and Sofia Coppola her Louis Vuitton luggage. I yawn with indifference every time I come across such silliness, but only seconds later find myself mentally going down my own list: my 24-inch iMac, my Octopus card, extra virgin olive oil... And of course, the daily delivery of *The International Herald Tribune*.

The *IHT*, the global edition of *The New York Times*, is hands down my favorite news source. Averaging only 18 pages, the newspaper can be read cover-to-cover in a single sitting. From politics and business to travels and arts and entertainment, "all the news that's fit to print" is packed into a single fold. The paper's editorials, written with old-fashioned gumption, always pack a punch. Daily crossword puzzles edited by word wizard Will Shortz get progressively difficult as the week matures and provide a work-out for the brain that at once entertains and humbles. Award-winning columnists like Alice Rawsthorn and Roger Cohen and sections with such enticing titles as "International Life" delight as much as they inspire. Whether it is an article about the Singapore government's attempt to boost its citizens' sex drive or a vignette on China's emerging middle class buying their first motor cars, the writing is superb and the research thorough.

On the other end of the spectrum are the local news media in Hong Kong. Unlike most other countries where sensationalism is limited to supermarket tabloids and gossip columns, in Hong Kong it appears impossible to sell a paper or magazine without an *exposé* on local celebrities, from a salacious sex act caught on amateur video to a teenage model accidentally exposing herself at a media event. Men and women, regardless of age, education, occupation and socio-economic class, devour the same *risqué* weeklies on the subway train or in a crowded restaurant with complete nonchalance. Anywhere else in the world, the reader would have been shamed by dirty looks from onlookers. Not here! The old adage that "you are what you read" has yet to get any traction among the local population.

Besides having to satisfy a sensation-hungry public, the Hong Kong press is suffering from a case of disappearing backbone. Ever since the 1997 handover, civil liberties in our city have been ebbing away in all aspects of life, but none more disconcerting than the freedom of expression. The erosion is never as overt as a violent crackdown or jailing of dissenters (those only happen *inside* China), but rather in the more subtle, tortuous form of self-censorship. Fearing the loss of advertising dollars, newspapers and magazines have grown increasingly gun shy about criticizing Beijing, and even complaints against our local government have lost their bite over the years. Every editorial, presumably the soul of a newspaper, disgorges toothless, self-evident commentary on the city's daily events, avoiding controversies of any kind. Commenting on the swine flu outbreak, for example, one newspaper urged the health department to be more vigilant to prevent an all-out epidemic. Do we really need an editorial to tell us that? Remarking on the Chinese Vice President's recent visit to Hong Kong, another newspaper asked the reader to put politics aside and work with Beijing to fight the global recession. Mr. Editor, you might want to wipe the brown off your nose.

While the city is asleep, the watchdogs are being quietly put down and the gadflies secretly swatted. Without a functioning Fourth Estate, Hong Kong is in serious danger of turning into another Singapore. Let's pray that that day will never come.

每天的困惑 Daily Conundrum

Every weekday at roughly the same time, when the Hong Kong market is about to take its mid-day break, a recurring question pops into my head and gives me an instant migraine. Tackling this question requires creativity and the ability to work through an intricate matrix of parameters: timing, budget, location, weather and mood. It has nothing to do with finance, accounting or the law. It's the eternal question of what's for lunch.

To most worker bees, lunch is a welcome break in an otherwise never-ending day and a source of relaxation or gastronomical indulgence. To this picky eater, however, the mere mention of the word makes his head throb. Every day at the dreaded lunch hour, I find myself out of options and out of time.

My office is at IFC Two. During the busy lunch hours from 12:30 to 2:00, the only way to get yourself inside an elevator is to travel up and wait for the jam-packed cage to hobble down floor by floor, literally taking 20 minutes just to get from your office to the lobby. And when the elevator finally releases its captives, the eternal question becomes an admission of defeat: there is nothing to eat around here!

The 88-story office tower rises above a glitzy, four-level shopping center. Too bad glitz doesn't fill the stomach. Most of the restaurants in the megamall, such as Isola, Inagiku and the snooty newcomer Agnès b. Le Pain Grillé, charge exorbitant prices for just a quick bite, making them utterly irrelevant to the average salary man. These permanent space-holders might as well swap their menus for monkey brains and bull testicles and it wouldn't affect us one bit.

Most large companies in other big cities operate in-house cafeterias offering a square meal at subsidized prices. My old law firm in New York has one, and so do my current employer's branches in London and Paris. Afraid of offending our capitalistic sensibilities with a communal dining facility, none of the corporate tenants at the IFC offers the amenity. The closest thing to a cafeteria here was the aptly-named Canteen, a self-service restaurant that served a variety of Asian and Western fare. That was until they were kicked out a year ago to make room for a mysterious "bread and wine bar" expected to open later this year. The "wine bar" bit certainly piques our suspicion. The last thing we need is another *tai tai* hangout while office-workers scour the mall for affordable food like raccoons in a garbage dump.

There are a number of practical eateries at the IFC, but only if you like salads or sandwiches. Call me old-fashioned, but I always need something warm in my stomach to get through a long day.

No amount of mixing and tossing of lettuce and cucumber can replace a proper warm meal. Apparently I am not the only one who thinks that. Just last week I caught three young men, each wearing an orange hat and white polo-shirt, sneaking out of McDonald's carrying bags full of burgers enough to feed a dozen people. They all worked at a new salad joint called Dressed Salads that opened last month on Level 2 of the IFC Mall. It seems that whatever free food their employer provided just didn't do it for them. Perhaps Dressed Salads should consider a policy against staff buying outside food while wearing company uniform.

I find sandwiches equally unappetizing. Lured by those neat triangular boxes, I have walked into Pret A Manger many times and ended up walking out empty-handed. The sandwiches with crusted bread – a big turnoff for me – and skimpy fillings are pre-made and refrigerated. But a dull sandwich still beats the artery-clogging burger, which packs a one-two punch of carbohydrates and fat. I am convinced that a four-inch thick whopper from Triple O's has enough calories to heat up a small apartment.

How about venturing outside the IFC? To be fair, there is no shortage of *cha chaan teng* (茶餐廳) local cafés and noodle houses along Stanley and Wellington Streets. The food is good and the prices are even better. But as anyone who works in Central would tell you, the queue to get in anywhere during lunch hours is deadly. Getting a seat at a shared table with six slurping strangers is like fighting a guerilla war in the Nicaraguan jungle. It demands perseverance and a strong elbow.

These days, good old Café de Coral (大家樂), a home-grown fast food chain operating since 1969, is a quick and dependable fix to my daily conundrum. Their lunch boxes, at a bargain price of HK$30 (less than US$4.00) a pop, are every bit as delicious as anything a fancy restaurant serves. Among my favorites are their signature roasted pork chop and beef brisket curry. The folksy restaurant with a folksy name is also remarkably efficient, with a behind-the-counter assembly line that would have impressed even Henry Ford. It never ceases to amaze me to watch the perfectly choreographed staff clear a long queue of customers within minutes. So what if their food is laced with MSG and made from dubious ingredients from China? So is everything else in Hong Kong nowadays.

A name Hong Kongers can count on for a scrumptious,
affordable meal

渡過金融海嘯

Riding out the Tsunami

I

There is a new expression in the U.S. "That's so August of you" is a jab at people who continue to spend lavishly during what has been touted as the greatest financial crisis since the Great Depression. For too long, Americans have been sleepwalking through life in the shopping mall, their bank accounts ebbing and flowing through the credit card billing cycle. From the gas-guzzling SUV to the fancy kitchen remodeling, every expense is put on the credit card or financed with a second home mortgage.

"Spend within your means" is an axiom that has gone unheeded for generations.

The world's wealthiest country has a long and dysfunctional love affair with plastic. The credit card is at once a symbol of high-rolling panache and a fuel for irresponsible spending. The spendthrift American drowning in credit card debt is the cultural equivalent of the stereotypical Chinese gambler. Whereas in Hong Kong we joke about young women who spend their entire monthly salary on a Louis Vuitton handbag, their American counterparts can easily rack up three times as much on their credit cards and no one bats an eye. And while Hong Kongers carry multiple credit cards in their wallets for the garden variety of retail discounts and reward programs they offered, Americans do so for a reason far less benign than ours: to tap a ready source of financing.

On average, an American household carries over US$10,000 in credit card debt spread over eight or nine different cards. Years ago, a friend of mine in New York told me she had just spent US$5,000 on a nose job, money she did not have. Her plan was to get as many credit cards that offered a 0% introductory APR as she could, and then transfer the balance from one card to the next once the interest-free period ran out. But things don't always work out the way we plan them, even for the savviest consumers among us. My friend ended up paying through the nose (so to speak) after she missed several monthly payments and got slammed with a usurial 44.99% finance charge. All in all, it took her three years to crawl out of the financial quicksand.

But the housing market meltdown has shaken a nation of shopaholics to the core, forcing its suddenly deflated citizens to take a hard look at their spending habits and to examine what really matters to them in life. Back in summer 2008, you couldn't get people to stop talking about getting that third family car or which boarding school in Europe to send their children to. Today, those bull market follies are not only reckless (if you can still afford them), but also decidedly uncool. AIG and Bernie Madoff uncool. On the other hand, behavior that was once considered "beneath ourselves," such as asking for a doggy bag at a restaurant or taking your clothes to the tailor's instead of buying new ones, will earn you kudos in today's topsy-turvy world. While textbooks on consumer psychology are being re-written, old virtues like humility and frugality have come back in vogue. The dark cloud that hangs over America, it seems, is not without its silver lining.

Buoyed by China's still-growing economy, this part of Asia has so far managed to stay relatively unscathed by the "financial tsunami," a new term coined by the local news media. While expatriates are leaving Singapore in droves and high-end malls in Bangkok have become marbled ghost towns, eager patrons continue to line up outside upscale restaurants and luxury stores in Hong Kong and Shanghai. Signs of a global recession in full swing are noticeably absent, making it easy for us to forget just how terrible things really are on the other side of the globe. In fact, many in China still believe that the current economic woes are merely an "American" problem, much the same way they looked at the 9-11 terrorist attacks.

Whether this sense of immunity is well-founded or naïve, and whether China, a country whose exports reportedly represent 40% of its GDP, is indeed fire-walled from the economic troubles across the Pacific, remain anyone's guess. But one thing is certain: China's industrial gravy-train is still going full steam ahead. As for the speck of land that is Hong Kong, we are holding our collective breath that the Mother Train will give us a free ride and deliver us out of the tsunami.

II

The global recession has come upon us and no one is spared. Stock prices around the world, having lost over half of their value since November 2007, have recovered somewhat in the past twelve months. But experts are calling it a "bear market rally" and warn of a calamitous double-dip recession. As the news media continue to stoke recessionary fears, at some point even the most defiant and deterministic among us must yield to the grim economic outlook we face. If this turn of events were God's way of testing our faith, then by setting off the financial market dominoes at the height of globalization, He sure has succeeded in bringing the rich and the poor, the famous and the unknown, the powerful and the meek all to their knees. Locusts, boils and death of the first-born are so 2000 B.C.!

Whatever our religious beliefs are, each one of us is trying to get through these tough times in our own way. Some choose to stay a little later in the office every night to prove themselves indispensable, while others decide to live under self-imposed house arrest and cut all non-essential spending. But life without an occasional splurge can get a little dull. The truth is, we have been spoiled by decades of continued economic growth, so spoiled that we have forgotten how to have fun without inflicting the sadomasochistic pain of hurting our own wallets. Consumption has become a necessary condition, sometimes even a sufficient condition, for enjoyment. But as my mother always says: the best things in life often cost the least. To prove her right, I am sharing my thoughts on how to have a jolly good time in Hong Kong without breaking the piggy bank. I call it "Jason's Day of Fun on a Shoestring."

A distraught investor during the market crash in November 2007

Start the day in Repulse Bay. Pack a beach towel, a couple of champagne flutes and a pocket knife. The scenic and comfortable bus ride from Central takes about half an hour and costs HK$8. Before you board the roaring double-decker, stop by the local grocery store and pick up a bottle of very drinkable Artelatino cava brut (HK$49), a wedge of inexpensive brie (around HK$35 depending on the weight) and a box of crackers (HK$15). Once there, find yourself a patch of soft sand and enjoy a generous dose of Vitamin D, nature's best anti-depressant. At the same time, pamper yourself with the affordable luxury of sparkling wine and soft cheese melting in the soothing sun. If that's not enough to fill the stomach, grab a couple of green apples and peanut butter – they make a killer snack.

After rinsing off the sand at the showers by the beach, take the bus back to Central and spend the afternoon at the MIX Juice Bar on Hollywood Road. A large "Blueberry More" smoothie with added ginger (HK$44), my favorite milk-free drink there, is the perfect act to follow a morning of solar exposure. Sitting by the floor-to-ceiling window and under the imitation Arco lamp, you get a maximum view of the colorful crowds traveling up and down the longest outdoor escalator system in the world. Once you have had enough people-watching, tune out the world with your iPod and read the weekend edition of your favorite newspaper from cover to cover or finish half of that Ian McEwan or Eileen Chang (張愛玲) novel. Two weeks ago I sat by that very window writing my new article about a recent trip to Bangkok and walked out four hours later feeling relaxed, recharged and enormously accomplished.

When the sun is just about to set, head down to the delightfully authentic Graham Street wet markets. Grocery shopping at the markets is an activity to savor slowly, for every corner offers a photo opportunity and each turn reveals a surprise. Alas, this last vestige of old Hong Kong has been slated for redevelopment and is facing demolition despite vehement opposition from local retailers and preservationists. So while this piece of edible history is still with us, take advantage of it and get everything you need for a simple and nutritious three-course dinner for two: a pound of greasyback shrimp (基圍蝦) for appetizer, chicken tenderloins and farm vegetables for a delectable stir-fry and fresh seasonal fruits for dessert. Live shrimp, trapped in makeshift fish-tanks made from shallow Styrofoam boxes and priced at HK$30 a pound, are guaranteed to be dancing in that pink plastic bag all the way to your kitchen sink. Blanch the jumpy crustaceans in a pot of boiling water for no more than 60 seconds and treat yourself to a plate of restaurant-quality steamed shrimp.

I have followed this routine dozens of times and it never gets old. The one-day program is economical, flexible and wonderfully scalable. You can choose to do it by yourself, with your loved one or with any number of friends. And don't let the weather tell you what you can or cannot do. Even on a rainy day, nothing should stop you from heading to the beach and reading a book under a canvas canopy along the boardwalk. The symphony of raindrops and ocean waves simply makes for a different kind of day, but a respite from your urban anxieties just the same. In these tumultuous times, staying positive and being adaptable is the only sure way of survival. As the cliché goes: if life gives you lemons, make lemonade.

百貨公司文化

Department Store Culture

Back in my school days in Philadelphia, The Wanamaker's, founded by prominent merchant and politician John Wanamaker in 1902, was among my favorite places to hang out in the downtown area. Every Christmas the department store delighted children and adults alike with an in-store light show while holiday tunes played beautifully on the world's largest operational pipe organ housed inside a majestic, seven-story high courtyard. Unfortunately for Philadelphians, as the department store industry waned, the iconic retailer eventually succumbed to changing times and in

1997, the century-old Wanamaker's name was taken down from one of the city's most prominent landmarks.

Once a social institution, department stores around the world are facing extinction. The rise of the "big-box store" that specializes in a single category of merchandise, such as office supplies, toys, footwear and sporting goods, has forever altered our shopping habits and made it impossible for department stores to compete in either price or selection. Trying to be all things to all people, these retail dinosaurs end up pleasing nobody. Here in Hong Kong, one department store after another went out of business at the turn of the new millennium, each time leaving an ocular void in the neighborhood like the carcass of a sunken ocean-liner.

Corporate Darwinism aside, the Japanese department store culture has long been an integral part of Hong Kong's history. Back when the British colony was still coming of age, Daimaru (大丸) opened a store on Great George Street in Causeway Bay in 1960. Daimaru was the first Japanese department store to make landfall in Hong Kong and was at the time the city's largest and most glamorous retail store. Other Japanese heavy-weights like Isetan (伊勢丹), Matsuzakaya (松坂屋) and Mitsukoshi (三越) soon followed. With its nose in the air, high-end Takashimaya (高島屋) noticeably skipped Hong Kong and went to Singapore and Taipei instead.

During their heyday in the 70s and 80s, Japanese department stores in Hong Kong doted on their adoring fans and satisfied their every shopping need with an impossible array of goodies from toys and kitchen appliances to sporting goods and furniture. The moment you walked through those heavy swing doors, the humdrum of city life dissolved into a paradise of squeaky clean marble floors, red escalator handrails and smiley staff in color-coordinated uniforms. Every corner sparkled and every turn revealed a hidden surprise.

Sogo department store in the heart of Causeway Bay

One of my fondest childhood memories involved running through the spacious toy section of Mitsukoshi and snatching my favorite LEGO set off the shelf as a promised reward at the end of a school year. I still have those brick sets in the basement of my parents' house in Toronto. Every time I walked past the section of Hennessy Road where the venerable store once stood, I would gaze at what is now a boarded up construction site and remember these moments of absolute, unqualified happiness. But by the time I repatriated to Hong Kong in 2005, Mitsukoshi had already withered into a discount bazaar on which bargain hunters fed like a pack of hyenas. Its glory from yesteryear was long gone. Before the iron gate permanently came down on the ailing retailer three years ago, sentimental shoppers bade tearful farewell and took home its signature tricolor shopping bag as their only memento.

Today, Sogo (崇光), Jusco (吉之島) and Wing On (永安) are the last bastions of the department store culture in Hong Kong. Competitors like Seibu (西武), Lane Crawford, Marks & Spencer and Sincere (先施) have made a collective decision to focus only on apparel and cosmetics and occasionally dabble in home accessories. They are no longer department stores in the truest sense. The story of Sogo, ever the beacon of hope and prosperity in Causeway Bay, is rather interesting. After its Japanese parent company collapsed under mounting debt in 2000, Sogo was sold to a Hong Kong company and is run just like one. But while department stores continue to be an endangered species, Sogo bucked the trend in 2005 and opened a new Tsim Sha Tsui store with a coveted Salisbury Road address, offering proof of its defiance against economic odds.

The Japanese department store has left an indelible mark on our city. These foreign retailers carried Hong Kong through its formative years from a fledgling cottage industry economy in the 1960s to the region's top metropolis it is today. But these days, if you want to experience once more the magic of the retail paradise, you will have to take a short flight to Tokyo and spend an afternoon at a Takashimaya store where the elevator lady still takes a 90-degree bow to customers and stays head-down until they walk out of her sight.

疾
病
或
健
康

In Sickness or in Health

I

Earlier this month, an army of 450 volunteer doctors and dentists from Remote Area Medical, a non-profit group created to bring modern medicine to third world countries, took over a football stadium in Los Angeles, California, to treat thousands of Americans who otherwise could not afford health care. At the same time, in town-hall meetings around the country, angry constituents shouted at their congressmen against President Obama's initiative to bring health care to every American, calling his reform bill "socialist" and comparing the president to Adolf Hitler. Something doesn't add up.

My first brush with the infamous American health care system came when I went to college in Philadelphia. Among the dozens of forms I had to fill out during the orientation week was a declaration that I had purchased private medical insurance, without which I could not even register for class. I asked my room-mate Adam what all that fuss was about. After giving me a how-should-I-explain-this-to-a-foreigner look, Adam warned that if I had no insurance and got hit by a bus, the emergency room would either leave me for dead or stick me with a hospital bill so steep it would bankrupt my parents. I started to laugh, but the laugh was not returned. Adam was dead serious.

Seeing a doctor in America is like taking your car to the mechanic – you nod to whatever the guy says and pay whatever he demands. To be precise, your *insurance company* pays whatever the health care provider demands, assuming you are among the 60% of the population covered by employer-sponsored medical insurance. To rein in escalating health care costs, insurance companies created HMOs (health maintenance organizations) and PPOs (preferred provider organizations) and use their market power to negotiate lower fees from a network of affiliated doctors and hospitals. But the other 40% – the self-employed and the unemployed – aren't so lucky. They must purchase their own medical insurance that costs as much as US$13,000 a year for a family of four, when an average American household takes home less than US$30,000 after tax. Spending nearly half of a paycheck on insurance premiums is utterly unthinkable for anyone outside America.

It is therefore no surprise that so many Americans are uninsured. Today, an estimated 48 million, or almost one in every six Americans, are priced out of a medical system dominated by HMOs, PPOs and other three-letter acronyms. They are the people who camped out for days earlier this month outside the football stadium in Los Angeles waiting to have their first mammogram or their children's wisdom teeth taken out. Some of them had not seen a doctor or a dentist in decades. In the world's wealthiest nation, the uninsured live in constant fear, their own bodies ticking time bombs. All it takes is a mysterious lump on the neck, a bad fall in the bathtub or anything that requires surgery or hospitalization for an uninsured family to fall into financial ruin. At a time when the economy edges toward double-digit unemployment, parents are increasingly facing a Sophie's Choice of providing medical care for their family or keeping a roof over their heads. And so this is what I would say to every screaming anti-reformist in those heated town hall meetings: walk a mile in the shoes of the uninsured and you just might see things a little differently.

Even for the 250 million lucky Americans who do have health insurance, many end up paying hefty co-payments and deductibles, especially those requiring long-term care and expensive medication. That is *if* the claimants get reimbursed at all. In the David-versus-Goliath battles against insurance companies, medical claims are routinely denied due to so-called "pre-existing conditions," and pre-approvals for treatments are often rejected because they are deemed "medically unnecessary," "experimental" or "investigational." In America, opening the ominous white envelope from an HMO can be one of the most harrowing experiences in life, for every denial letter is potentially a death sentence.

Today, the United States remains the only country in the industrialized world without universal health coverage. President Obama, determined to make good on his campaign promise to bring every citizen into the system, risked all his political capital by pushing an ambitious healthcare reform bill through Congress. Central to the bill was the so-called "public option" that would allow citizens to choose between a government-funded plan and private insurance. The public option was sometimes analogized to the government-run U.S. Postal Service that offers an affordable but still reliable alternative to private delivery services like FedEx and DHL. In fact, America is no stranger to nationalized, single-payer health care. For over 40 years, the U.S. government has been running Medicaid for people over the age of 65 and Medicare for certain eligible low-income citizens, as well as providing free care for military personnel and veterans.

Obama's reform initiative was at once a noble cause, a political gamble and a lightning rod for partisan criticisms. The reform bill sparked a national debate that divided the country along party lines. Where you stand on the issue depends on your income, age, health and, above all, your ideology. But in the eye of this social liberal, health care is a complex question with a surprisingly simple answer. It all comes down to one fundamental question: do you believe every citizen should have the right to health care? If we can't even agree on this question, then America has a much bigger problem than the one it is facing.

Obama's effort to reform the medical system was matched by equal determination by the Republicans to sabotage it, just as they did to Hillary Clinton in 1993 when she was First Lady and Health-Care-Reformist-in-Chief. This time around, the embattled Republican Party was using fear mongering, a tactic they had perfected during the Bush administration, to distract the public and to drown out rational debate. Conservatives spread rumors and invented horror stories about Obama's reform bill, including something called a "death panel" that would presumably allow the government to decide whether a patient lives or dies. Two weeks ago, the smear campaign spilled across the Atlantic after Republicans attacked Britain's popular National Health Service as an "evil" plan. Even Stephen Hawking, the renowned physicist who suffers from Lou Gehrig's disease, jumped into the fray to dispel outlandish claims that he "wouldn't have a chance" under the British system. All the while the world looked on, wondering how long this political circus will go on before Americans get serious about catching up with the rest of the industrialized world on health care.

The health care reform bill was eventually passed this past December, although not a single Republican voted in favor of it. In the nick of time, President Obama was forced to drop the public option to get the job done, making it a Pyrrhic Victory for the Obama administration as the bill fell way short of providing universal health care to all Americans. Over the course of its history, the United States has time and again shown the world that it is capable of doing the right thing for its people even in the toughest and most improbable of moments, from the abolition of slavery to the election of an African-American president. The 2010 health care reform was not one of those moments.

II

Several months ago a good friend of mine in Hong Kong had a medical emergency. Struck suddenly by paralyzing stomach pain, Wilson checked himself into Hong Kong Sanatorium & Hospital (養和醫院) in Happy Valley. He underwent surgery the following day and remained hospitalized for a week. Luckily for Wilson, his company's medical plan covered a big part of his hospital bill and whatever extra charges for staying in a swanky semi-private ward were picked up by the supplemental insurance my friend had purchased on his own. Fully recovered and feeling quite pampered, Wilson walked out of the Sanatorium seven days later with a new found zest for life.

Sickness, like natural disasters and death, is a powerful leveler of mankind. Sure enough, Wilson's health scare struck him without warning and brought his busy life to a complete halt. His experience was a sobering reminder to everyone around him that good health is as fragile as bad health is non-negotiable. The day after I learned of Wilson's story, I called up an insurance agent and signed up for my own supplemental medical insurance. It was one of those expenses that one shouldn't spare.

Queen Mary Hospital in Pokfulam

In Hong Kong, a place where public education and social security leave much to be desired, our health care system is surprisingly robust. There are a dozen private hospitals and around 50 public hospitals scattered all over the city. Public hospitals are operated and funded by the Hospital Authority created two decades ago to improve management and oversight. The most comforting part about Wilson's story is that he could have gone to any one of the public hospitals in the city and he wouldn't have been any worse off. Public hospitals like Queen Mary Hospital (瑪麗醫院) in Pokfulam dispense world-class care and boast many of the region's top medical specialists and researchers. What's more, universal coverage in Hong Kong means that my friend would have paid close to nothing for his surgery and hospital stay, a rare bargain in an otherwise penny-pinching society.

Hong Kong's health care system is similar to that in other Asian countries and most of Europe, where free, government-funded medical care co-exists with private health services. Canada, Australia and Taiwan adopted a slightly different system, under which doctors in public hospitals and private practice are both paid by the government (and hence the term "single payer system"), thereby leveling the pay-scale and balancing the supply of medical professionals in both sectors.

Most people in Hong Kong go to private doctors for out-patient care such as treating a seasonal flu or a persistent cough. A visit sets the patient back around HK$200 (US$25), if he is not otherwise reimbursed by his group medical plan at work. As for in-patient care like what Wilson received at the Sanatorium, the choice between private and public care becomes more real and the patient's decision comes down to his insurance coverage and personal preference. In Wilson's case, he chose a private hospital not because he expected better-skilled surgeons there, but rather because the wards are less crowded and the doctors tend to make more frequent rounds. In the grand scheme of things, however, those are mere icing-on-the-cake that most people can probably live without.

For emergency services such as trauma care for victims involved in serious traffic accidents, the ambulance will invariably take them directly to the nearest public hospital. Exclusive and pampering as our private hospitals are, none of them have the capabilities to handle patients requiring urgent medical treatment. It was a lesson I learned the hard way two years ago when I took another friend of mine with a bad case of ear infection to Canossa Hospital (嘉諾撒醫院) in Midlevels, only to be turned away by the GP on duty who eagerly gave us the address of the nearby public hospital. All in all, government-run hospitals in Hong Kong are reliable, well-managed and a source of solace and pride for the seven million who depend on them.

But solace and pride are in short supply these days. A series of medical blunders at the city's flagship public hospitals have shaken the Hospital Authority to the core and caused an instant media frenzy. Last month, a breast cancer patient at North District Hospital (北區醫院) in Sheung Shui was mistakenly injected with 2.5 grams of oral morphine. Within the same month, nurses at Queen Elizabeth Hospital (伊利沙伯醫院) in King's Park mixed up the identity bracelets of a pair of newborns and the mothers ended up breast-feeding each other's baby for five days. Just last week, Queen Elizabeth Hospital was in the news again for giving five infants expired BCG vaccinations. The series of unfortunate events are at best isolated incidents caused by uneliminable risks inherent in every medical system. At worst, they are signs that our system is becoming over-strained and sclerotic, raising questions about the sustainability of a government-funded system in face of an ever aging population.

Hong Kong's health care system is not perfect. But it delivers what the city needs and leaves no one out in the cold. The system we have reflects our collective belief that health care is a fundamental, inalienable right to which every citizen is entitled. That is more than one can say about America, a leader in virtually every aspect of life except for the one that matters most. When it comes to the issue of health care access, the United States has much to learn from just about every country on the planet.

Flip-flops Culture

A good friend of mine once observed, there are only three kinds of men who wear flip-flops in Hong Kong: street bums, foreigners and homosexuals.

I suspect the marginalization of this simple, versatile and very comfortable footwear has much to do with language. In Cantonese, as it is the case for Thai, Vietnamese and several other Asian languages I have surveyed, there is no specific word for flip-flops. All open-toe footwear held with a thong between the big toe and the second toe is generically referred to as "slippers" (拖鞋), a word that strongly suggests its rightful place in the privacy of one's own home. Likewise, the Cantonese word for "vest" (背心) can mean anything from the sleeveless member of a three-piece suit to a tank-top or a cardigan, a term that often causes confusion at clothing stores in the city.

I love flip-flops and I wear them everywhere I go. Over the years, my trusty flip-flops have taken me to the backstreets of Harlem, Mount Fuji in Japan and recently the Great Wall of China. In subtropical Hong Kong, I can be seen wearing the rubbery footwear all year round, strolling through the slippery wet markets on Graham Street or window shopping at the glitzy Landmark mall. I was once told that it is against the law in Hong Kong to drive wearing flip-flops because of their tendency to slip off your feet, even though I figure the risk of having my feet checked by a policeman on an expressway is really quite remote. But just to avoid any trouble with the law, I often drive barefoot instead, which is legal.

Ever since I moved to Hong Kong from New York City four years ago, not a weekend has gone by without someone commenting on my flip-flops with curiosity, disapproval or both. Some of the common reactions I get are "how was the beach?" (even though it was in the middle of winter), "you must live very close by!" (implying that I didn't bother to change when I left the apartment) and, my favorite of them all, "oh, how casual..." Translation: have some respect and cover your toes!

Curiously enough, flip-flops in Hong Kong are much more than just footwear. For instance, they are the weapon of choice against the ubiquitous cockroach in the humid summer months. A trained killer can kick the piece of rubber off his foot into his ready hand and send it flying in a spinning trajectory until it lands on the target with a decisive "clop" – all within a split second of spotting the brown critter that never stands a chance. Besides being a handy weapon, flip-flops are an essential part of the Chinese voodoo kit used by those old ladies hired to chant curses against a hated relative or a romantic rival. You can catch a glimpse of this traditional form of witchcraft under the Canal Road Flyover (鵝頸橋) in Wanchai. These days, however, you will find that many of the practitioners have traded the flip-flop for a high-heel to pack a spikier punch. Just the same, it is fascinating to watch those otherwise innocent-looking women dish out rancorous rhymes against total strangers. I can't help but wonder who actually hires them and how much they charge. I don't suggest you ask them.

Modern day witchcraft on full display in Wanchai

I don't know what it would take for Asia to finally accept flip-flops as a fashion statement for men. But one thing is for sure: they have been a cultural icon in Hong Kong long before they became popular in the West.

香港過聖誕

Christmas in Hong Kong

I

My seven-and-a-half foot tall Oregon Douglas fir arrived today. I only just picked it out from the florist's yesterday, but with typical Hong Kong efficiency, the perfectly wrapped tree, complete with a tree stand and accessories, was delivered to my apartment in less than 24 hours. Unwrapping the tree was every bit as exciting as opening presents on Christmas Day. And as soon as the bunched-up branches were released, they let out an aroma of fresh pine that permeated the entire living room, instantly triggering wonderful olfactory memories of past Christmases.

A real Christmas tree can instantly enliven a living room

I had a real tree for Christmas in all my years in New York and have had one ever since I returned to Hong Kong. In Manhattan, tree vendors pop up on every street corner as soon as Thanksgiving is over. Most of them are Canadians who drive their pick-up trucks from up north in hope of making a holiday buck over the December weeks. One year I bought a five-foot Canadian spruce from a Quebecois lady from Montreal and we talked for a good half-hour in the freezing cold before I took home the beautiful tree. There is nothing like curling up on the sofa with a hot cup of apple cider and admiring a handsome tree wrapped in twinkling lights when, outside the frosty window, the first snow flakes just begin to fall.

Back in New York, I used to go tree-shopping with my brother Dan every year in early December. The experience is likened to visiting the Victoria Park flower markets in Hong Kong during Chinese New Year, minus the dizzying crowds and the screaming teenage entrepreneurs. Back in those days, Dan and I would keep the trees in our respective apartments until as late as Valentine's Day. One of the great things about living in Manhattan is that once you are done with the old tree, you can simply leave it out on the street to be picked up by the dutiful garbage collectors. And so every year, around mid-January, you will see abandoned Christmas trees piled up on sidewalks all over the city.

One of the funniest Christmas stories I know involved Dan buying a tree from the neighborhood deli – a deli is equivalent to a convenient store in Hong Kong – on his own. Neither his wife nor I was there to offer a second opinion and my brother took home a sad-looking skeleton of a plant, droopy branches and all. For days we teased him about his bad purchase until he finally threw the tree out the night before Christmas and scrambled to buy a replacement just hours before vendors disappeared for the year. I told him that he was probably the first and the only person in the entire history of America to toss out a Christmas tree on Christmas Eve. True enough, every time we walked down 16th Street where he lived, we would see the abandoned tree lying prostrate on the sidewalk and hear mumblings from passersby who gawked at the odd sight. Dan would whisper to me sheepishly, "just look away and keep walking!"

I haven't started trimming or decorating my new Christmas tree. I will give it a day or two and let gravity do its work on the branches. Putting up lights and ornaments is as much a science as it is an art. The decorator must assess how many sparkly things he has at his disposal and space them perfectly over the branches, but not *too* perfectly or else the arrangement lacks imagination.

One wrong move and he may have to start all over again. It can be quite a chore, but it's one that very few of us mind doing.

II

This is my fourth Christmas in Hong Kong since I left New York. These days Christmas is more commonly referred to as the "holiday season" to make non-Christians feel less excluded from the festivities. It is part of the "political correctness" movement that began in America in the 1990s and forever altered the way Americans conduct themselves and interact with each other. The name change is a harmless adjustment that has done little to dampen the holiday spirit. After all, it will not stop little children from taking pictures with Santa Claus at the mall or party-goers from guzzling champagne.

The absence of snow in Hong Kong, on the other hand, does put a damper on things. That perhaps explains why Hong Kongers felt the need to develop our own peculiar way of celebrating the occasion. For starters, it is a tradition here for friends and family to swamp five-star hotel restaurants for their annual Christmas Eve dinner buffet. The meal is just an excuse to gorge on lobsters, oysters and sushi, none of which is part of the classic Christmas fare. Hotels use these expensive items to lure customers who demand the biggest bang for their buck. But thanks to this odd tradition, food poisoning cases surge in December year after year, as weak stomachs give out to hastily ingested seafood of inferior quality, chosen by restaurant kitchens determined to outmaneuver their penny-smart customers.

In the Western Hemisphere, holiday revelers party hard on New Year's Eve. December 24, on the other hand, is reserved for family and loved ones to have an intimate dinner at home.

Many Hong Kong tourists learn this cultural lesson the hard way when they time their trip just so they can spend Christmas Eve in New York or Paris, only to find closed stores and deserted streets everywhere and end up ordering room service in their hotel rooms. This misunderstanding exists for the most part because the holiday calendar in Hong Kong is off by a week. Party-goers here jump the gun and throw street parties on Christmas Eve, creating a bizarre custom called the "Christmas countdown." *Three, two, one... Merry Christmas!* The bells toll twelve times and everyone blows their party squawkers to a holiday frenzy. The scene is straight out of *Ripley's Believe It or Not*, for no one else in the world believes that the birth of baby Jesus needs to be rung in. Worse, many of these silly countdowns are official events organized by the government. You would think that someone in the rank-and-file would have the good sense to raise a red flag and put a stop to the madness. It is truly an "only in Hong Kong" moment.

Cultural oddities aside, what irks me the most about spending Christmas in Hong Kong is the noticeable absence of Christmas spirit. I am referring to those magical moments in December when everyone suddenly becomes a little friendlier and more generous. During those snowy winter weeks in New York, for instance, time-pressed shoppers pause to pick up an extra gift for a neighborhood toy drive, perfect strangers pay for each other's coffee at the drive-through and children empty their piggy-banks into the Salvation Army donation box. When you start to feel that warmth in the air, you know Christmas is just around the corner.

On the other hand, Christmas in Hong Kong – and in Asia for that matter – is all about shopping. December is merely the month for retail stores to clear their fall inventory and an excuse for shoppers to blow their year-end bonuses on things they don't need. It's not hard to understand why. Christmas has never been, and is still not, an official holiday in many Asian countries, including Mainland China, Japan, Thailand and Vietnam. In Hong Kong, even though citizens have long embraced the holiday after it was first introduced to the city by colonial Britain a century and a half ago, their appreciation of it remains on a superficial level. The deeper, more cultural elements, on the other hand, have fallen by the wayside. I often compare Christmas in Hong Kong to Chinese New Year in San Francisco: no matter how much a white American family enjoys lion dances and turnip cakes, it is difficult for them to fully understand the sense of renewal, hope and reflection that comes with the Spring Festival. Over the years, I have come to accept Christmas in Hong Kong as something that only looks pretty on the outside and has not much to look at on the inside.

Halfway through my Christmas shopping in Causeway Bay, I decided to grab a bite at the Times Square food court. As I was wolfing down my fried noodles, a Mainland Chinese tourist walked past me and almost lost his balance juggling a heavy tray of food and several shopping bags. I leaped out of my seat to take his tray and set it on the table next to mine. He thanked me with a gentle smile. Fifteen minutes later, when the gentleman finished his meal, he got up, looked me in the eye and said *xie-xie, xie-xie*, nodding profusely. His genuine gratitude over my insignificant act of kindness moved me deeply. Have I just been proven wrong? Perhaps Christmas spirit does exist here after all, and it will find you when you least expect it.

Part 3
The Places We Go

Tokyo Impressions

I spent a week in Tokyo last month as part of my twice-annual pilgrimage to one of my favorite cities. Like many in Hong Kong, I take guilty pleasure in all things Japanese. Saddled by the burden of history, all ethnic Chinese in my generation are taught to loathe the Japanese or at least keep them at bay. How we are to separate our sworn enemies' heinous past from their admirable qualities continues to elude every Japanophile among us.

Moral dilemmas aside, I find the Japanese aesthetics irresistible. The marriage of Shintoism and *Zen* Buddhism has produced such core values as *wabi* (侘; simplicity and transience) and *sabi* (寂; beauty of age and time). They are the underpinnings of every aspect of the Japanese culture from theater and architecture to food preparation and social etiquette. A perfect storm was formed when these values collided with *bushido* (武士道), the strict code of conduct of the *samurai* warrior, resulting in an idiosyncrasy that is exacting, nuanced and immensely graceful. At once a philosophy and a national identity, the Japanese aesthetics make even the most mundane of activities, such as cooking a bowl of *udon* or gift-wrapping a box of rice crackers, a ceremonial ritual to behold and admire.

I checked into my usual hotel in the Nihonbashi (日本橋) area and was led to the familiar room by a porter of impeccable manners. Ensconced on the 36th floor, I sat by the floor-to-ceiling window and looked out to the west side of the capital city as the winter sun began to set. The endless ocean of concrete buildings outside the window would have made for a rather austere sight if not for the countering tranquility supplied by the majestic Mount Fuji, the snow-capped symbol of Japan known for its perfect symmetry and understated grace. I rested my cup of *sencha* (煎茶) on the window sill and concluded that balance and moderation, the state of mind sought by every Japanese, must be as ubiquitous as vending machines in this country.

I was to meet up with a few friends for supper in Shinjuku (新宿) and I decided to take the subway like everyone else. During the evening rush hours, the streets remained eerily quiet despite the heavy pedestrian traffic, a testament to the people's self-restraint and non-intrusive nature. I stepped onto the subway train and wedged myself among scores of primly dressed citizens. As endless public announcements in melodious Japanese and accented English filled the silence, I scanned the sea of faces around me. Japan boasts one of the world's largest middle-class populations. A vast majority of its people enjoy a similar standard of living, leaving little reason for anyone to show off or envy. The country's even distribution of wealth is in stark contrast to the economic divide in the rest of Asia. In Hong Kong, and much more so in China and other emerging economies in the region, income inequality remains the greatest polarizing force in societies, and the tension between the haves and the have-nots continues to breed greed, envy, wrath and other deadly sins. Fifty feet below ground in bustling Tokyo, I found myself suddenly overcome with melancholy.

Dizzying streets of Tokyo

At Omotesando (表参道), one of the busiest subway stations, the train doors opened and disgorged herds of weary passengers of identical countenance. Seemingly content with their places in society, working men and women dress alike, eat similar foods and amuse themselves with the same pastimes. Conformism, the quintessential Japanese trait, is simultaneously the source of its people's greatest strength and their greatest weakness. Conformism gave Japan the social cohesion to rise from feudal poverty after the Meiji Restoration (明治維新) and to rebuild a devastated nation after World War II. But the same trait also put the country on the gruesome path of aggression in the first half of the 20th Century and left it toiling in the Lost Decade of economic stagflation in the 1990s. Today, conformism continues to keep Japan a largely closed society, impenetrable to immigrants and expatriates uniformly branded as *gaijin* (外人). Tokyo may be neck-and-neck with New York for the title of the world's greatest city. But what the Big Apple lacks in modernity and infrastructure, it makes up for in its ability to attract top talent from every corner of the world, allowing the city to constantly re-invent itself. New York's porosity is something that xenophobic Tokyo, despite all its glitz and glitter, can never measure up to.

I stepped out of the subway train at Shinjuku station and met up with my friends before we settled into our favorite *izakaya* (居酒屋; wine bar) a few city blocks away. With good food, good company and a constant supply of *yakitori* and *sake*, it was impossible not to have a good time. As we ate and drank our night away, I noticed quite a number of empty tables around us. The ominous signs of a deep recession were everywhere, but none more noticeable than the disappearance of the evening restaurant crowds. The long line of eager customers formed outside the bar had been replaced by a smiley waiter waving the *sake* menu at each passer-by. The world's second-going-on-third-largest economy has been hit hard by the global financial meltdown. A country of lifetime employment and corporate paternalism, Japan is witnessing an increasing number of laid-off workers facing unemployment and even homelessness. As I finished my last cup of rice wine for the night, I couldn't help but wonder whether conformism would once again deliver the country from its dire straits or push it even deeper into decline.

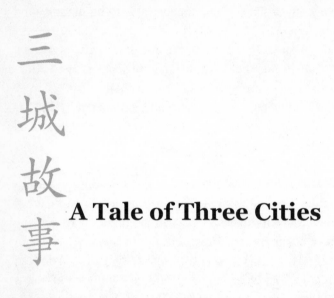

A Tale of Three Cities

Shenzhen, Macau and Hong Kong are three sisters separated in childhood. Tucked away in the Pearl River Delta, they might have been mistaken for triplets if it weren't for the vicissitudes of history that put them on such different paths. A century and a half ago, armed strangers came knocking on their door in the dead of night, waking the sleepers out of a national slumber. The mightiest among the intruders, bearing the Union Jack, snatched the oldest sister in the name of free trade, not long before a Latin *conquistador* ran off with the middle one. Their pillage and plunder would go on for several more decades before a new enemy brought on by a divine wind opened a chapter so dark history textbooks had to be revised.

Shenzhen

Good or bad, Shenzhen was the only sister of the three spared from colonial rule. While Hong Kong thrived under British rule and Portuguese Macau carved a niche for itself as Asia's Sin City, Shenzhen didn't begin to come of age until 1980 when Deng Xiaoping handpicked her to be China's first Special Economic Zone. A late bloomer notwithstanding, the southern belle flourished under the auspices of Deng's Reforms and Openness (改革開放) initiatives and quickly became a poster girl for the country's pragmatic socialism. For the most part, however, Shenzhen in the early years of her economic boom remained China's Wild Wild West where pickpockets roamed and urban legends of child abduction and organ theft swirled.

In the late 1990s, China celebrated the home-coming of Hong Kong and Macau, only to find the abductees emotionally attached to the kidnappers in a textbook case of Stockholm Syndrome. The two sisters bade tearful farewell to the European colonizers who modernized them and returned to a family they barely recognized. Decolonization had never been so sullen. Economically inferior and culturally worlds apart, Shenzhen looked on as the Westernized sisters came home, suddenly self-conscious of her own Chineseness.

Today, Shenzhen boasts her own international airport, subway system, stock exchange and a population larger than Hong Kong's. But next to her worldly if not somewhat whitewashed sisters, Shenzhen remains unmistakably Chinese. Loiterers squat outside hotels and shopping centers. Grown men in three-piece suits chew on sugar cane stalks and spit out the bagasse on the sidewalk. Store clerks hold up each money bill to the light to check for counterfeits and occasionally recycle them. Shenzhen has made great progress, but she is still a long way from becoming the kind of world metropolis she so aspires to be.

This past weekend my friends and I took a day trip to Shenzhen to get away from the humdrum of Hong Kong without having to deal with airports and planes. The Luohu (羅湖) checkpoint used to be a complete circus, but years of trial and error have made crossing the border positively uneventful. Gone are the days when brusque customs officers, garbed in menacing military uniform, threw your passport or home return permit (回鄉證) back at you and shouted "*xia yi ge*" (下一個; next in line) before there was enough time to move out of the way. Officers nowadays are efficient and courteous, in part because of the instant feedback machines placed right in front of them: press red for "dissatisfied," yellow for "satisfied" or green for "perfect."

I visit Shenzhen for its food and *tui na* (推拿; deep-tissue massage). To say nothing of their wallet-friendly prices, many of the city's fine Chinese restaurants would impress even the staunchest of skeptics. Jiangnan Chuzhu (江南廚子), a Hangzhou restaurant at the glitzy Mixc shopping center (萬象城), cooks up a tofu skin and dried ham soup so delicious each time it provokes a near-orgasmic reaction from this gastronome. Likewise, the city's many massage parlors are more hygienic and legitimate than rumors would have you believe. Seasoned therapists, mostly migrant workers from nearby provinces, rub, knead, slap and elbow with effortless precision. I never hesitate to use my limited Mandarin to strike up a conversation with my masseur and get myself a free lesson on Chinese ethnography.

Dafen Oil Painting Village (大芬油畫村) in the Longgang District (龍崗區) is as much a mecca for budding artists fresh out of university as it is for art-lovers priced out of traditional galleries. An army of mercenary painters will copy anything put in front of them, from the swirly Van Gogh masterpiece to the narcissistic four-framed Warhol'esque portrait we all secretly covet. International hotel chains buy their paintings by the container and ship them to every corner of the world before the paint even dries. A giant scroll of Chinese calligraphy I ordered from Dafen two years ago now proudly adorns the foyer of my apartment.

Hundreds of young graduates copying masterpieces in the oil painting village

Indeed, copying is what Shenzhen does best. More than a means of survival, it is the only way she knows to catch up with her two sisters. Every day, factories big and small reverse-engineer anything from mobile phones to designer furniture, supplying the rest of China with the latest consumer goods and polluting the streets of New York and Paris with knockoffs and counterfeits. Dongmen (東門), a sprawling marketplace in the Luohu District, is at once a giant factory outlet for shoppers and a sourcing depot for enterprises from around the world. "Hi-Phones" and "Prado" handbags fill the under-lit shopping arcades, while pirated DVDs hit the shelf before the movies reach the big screens. Flagrant copyright infringements fly in the face of world trade agreements, and the city makes Napster and BitTorrent look like amateurs.

Three decades into its Gold Rush, Shenzhen is still hyperventilating with double-digit growth, tempered but unfazed by the recent economic downturn. Fearless entrepreneurship and moral agnosticism continue to transform our sister city every day, for better or for worse. Like many of the products she makes, Shenzhen is a work-in-progress, nearly there but not quite, almost real but not exactly.

Macau

Macau is a rustic peninsula hugged by a muddy, silt-laden estuary of the Pearl River. Petite, laid-back and never prosperous, the middle sister exudes a touch of quaint Mediterrasian charm. In the mid-16th Century, Portuguese merchants turned the sleepy fishing village into a leading *entrepôt* for the silk and silver trades between Europe, China and Japan. But Macau's heyday lasted until 1842, when British-controlled Hong Kong, with a deeper harbor and better-run government, dethroned the sandy peninsula as the gateway to the Orient. From then on, Macau was relegated to the role of an adjunct city of Hong Kong and would forever live in her big sister's shadow.

In the post-war era, Macau survived on revenues from government-sanctioned gambling and the sex trade, making a name for herself as Asia's Las Vegas and a modern-day Sodom and Gomorrah. While casinos and brothels were keeping the city afloat, they did little to raise Macau's profile and were pushing her further into an economic *cul-de-sac*. Half-heartedly governed by faraway Portugal, the colony was run by *de facto* governor Stanley

Ho (何鴻燊), who reportedly owned 80% of the city. When China finally welcomed home the European-bred daughter in 1999, Macau was a city paralyzed by organized crime and mired in the Asian financial crisis. If only the Portuguese had taken the same care with Macau as the British did with Hong Kong! But then, with frightening efficiency, Beijing began cleaning up the streets, capturing and executing a handful of high-profile mafia kingpins. Order restored, Macau turned her attention to the city's sputtering economy.

In a history-making move, the Macanese government in 2002 ended Stanley Ho's decades-long monopoly in the gaming business and handed concessions and sub-concessions to a half-dozen foreign and Chinese companies. With the stroke of a pen, the government turned the 11-square-mile peninsula into a Casino Royale for six individuals to place bets on the city's future. Three Las Vegas casino czars, Steve Wynn, Sheldon Adelson and Kirk Kerkorian, faced off against Australia's richest man James Packer, Hong Kong industrialist Lui Che-Woo (呂志和) and, of course, Stanley Ho himself. Half a million Macanese people looked on, as their livelihood hung on the whims of a handful of billionaires.

Eager to check out the new developments in our sister city, last month I hopped onto a jetfoil and checked into the brand new Venetian, the largest hotel in the world, located on the strikingly artificial Cotai Strip (路氹金光大道). The 2,300-suite Goliath was packed with hordes of Mainland Chinese visitors determined to spend the weekend risking it all at the felted table. Since the handover, Macau has been a Venus Flytrap for Chinese government officials to flaunt and lose their new fortunes. Baccarat is their game of choice, accounting for 85% of all casino revenues in Macau. The game requires absolutely no skill, which suits the amateur gamblers just fine. But gambling without paid sex just seems a little drab. And so at any given casino resort in the city, clusters of prostitutes stand guard at every entrance while casino management looks the other way. As I walked through the smoke-filled gaming hall of the Venetian, I was accosted by umpteen streetwalkers straight from the *Pretty Woman* movie set. As if their *risqué* outfits weren't obvious enough, one of them let out a brusque "psst" and gave me a wink that made my hair stand on end.

I took a taxi to Largo do Senado (議事亭前地), the colorfully paved town center where quaint local shops have long given way to Starbucks and McDonalds. With my trusty Nikon in hand, I sauntered through the old city and photographed the stretch of colonial buildings between Rua Do Almirante Sergio (河邊新街) and Rua da Felicidade (福隆新街). From street signs to government documents, everything in the ex-colony must be translated and printed in Portuguese, all for the benefit of the 5% ethnic Portuguese and the handful of tourists from Portugal and Brazil. Charming and nostalgic as it once was, Portuguese-Chinese bilingualism seems somewhat silly in this day and age, if not downright cumbersome and costly.

From Largo do Senado I strolled down Avenida de Almeida Ribeiro (亞美打利庇盧大馬路), the main thoroughfare that connects the old town to the new, to pay respect to the pageantry of new casino resorts. Then suddenly I froze in pain, as if hit by a baseball bat right between the eyes. It was the hideous Grand Lisboa (新葡京) casino, Stanley Ho's latest project, years in the making. Despite its enormous budget and prime location, the design defies both reason and description. To take shelter from the ocular assault, I ran toward the monstrosity and rushed into the casino lobby. Inside the egg-shaped structure, ugliness explodes on every wall, ceiling and floor. Ho's personal collection of sculptures and artifacts are put on display against a backdrop of neo-Egyptian columns studded with palm-sized *faux* rubies and opals. Strands of crystal beads hang from every place possible. A Noah's Ark of tacky art, the Grand Lisboa is a fitting tribute to its owner: a flamboyant billionaire, a self-congratulating polygamist, an alleged gangster and, above all, a living example of the tasteless Asian tycoon.

The repulsive Grand Lisboa behind the old Lisboa Casino

Everywhere I went in Macau, I saw signs of an economy in peril. Construction has been halted for several high-profile projects and the streets are eerily quiet compared to during her boom years at the turn of the millennium. The global economic crisis, coupled with new visa restrictions from Beijing to crack down on officials who gamble away state funds, has threatened the very survival of a city that puts all her eggs in one basket. Macau is where the underworld becomes the upperworld, where casinos merrily collect life-savings from foolhardy gamblers and family men live out their sexual fantasies. In a symbolic journey Hong Kongers call *guo dai hoi* (過大海; literally, crossing the big sea), visitors cross the muddy waters to the underworld, lured by the middle sister who beckons like a siren singing in shadowy water.

Hong Kong

The first sunbeams pierce the morning fog and sweep across the island's verdant back. A lonesome streetcar emerges from the west praya, still dark in the shadow of the Peak, and rumbles noisily down the tracks. One by one congee shop owners push up their metal gates, not long before the sound of clanging crockery fills the dewy air. As the rising sun pours gold over the silver city, tree sparrows tweet to its quickening pulse and Hong Kong wakes up to another day.

If New York is the city that never sleeps, then Hong Kong must be the one that doesn't even blink. More so than its magnificent skyline or its dubious title as a shoppers' paradise, our inexhaustible energy is the single biggest attraction for visitors from around the world. The stereotypical Hong Konger is a souped-up Energizer Bunny clutching a Gucci handbag in one hand and the latest smart-phone in the other. Our unrelenting determination to out-do, out-smart and out-last each other, cut-throat though it may be, is at once the glue that holds us together and our only discernible cultural identity. It is what keeps a tenth-grader going to cram schools night after night and the wiry octogenarian pushing a cartful of scrap metal up the hilly streets come rain or shine. It is what makes the big sister absolutely irresistible.

The magnificent Hong Kong skyline

The fact is undisputed: Hong Kongers work hard, think fast and aim high. With an army of workaholics and go-getters, our city should have been at the pinnacle of human achievements, the sort of model society Adam Smith envisioned in *The Wealth of Nations*. But over a decade after the 1997 Handover, the big sister seems to be sitting on her "invisible hands" while fellow Asian Tigers re-invent themselves into technology powerhouses and cultural trendsetters.

Blame it on our government and the select few who run it. Visionless, self-righteous and out of touch, the bureaucratic machine mops up private sector rejects and rewards their holier-than-thou attitude with fat paychecks and lifetime employment known as the "iron rice bowl" (鐵飯碗) in the local vernacular. The head bureaucrat, our chief executive, is handpicked by Beijing to do only one thing: keep citizens off the streets. But after Beijing got burned by the politically radioactive Tung Chee-hwa (董建華), the city's first chief executive, party seniors turned to someone much safer and more predictable. Donald Tsang, a career civil servant reminiscent of the dutiful English butler, made for a perfect candidate as the next party mouthpiece and baby pacifier.

Under Tsang's playing-it-safe leadership, Hong Kong has fallen behind on almost every front. His predecessor's ambition of turning our city into Asia's Silicon Valley is now dead in the water, with Cyberport a glorified movie theater and Science Park just another commercial property with not much science or park. The Kai Tak Redevelopment Project (啟德發展計劃), promising to transform the defunct airport into a world class ocean terminal, is yet to see its first bulldozers after eleven years of planning and consultation. And where are we with air quality, education reform and soaring property prices? Tsang and his cabinet would rather sit on a HK$1.5 trillion (US$186 billion) foreign exchange reserve than spending some of it on our future, for one's money always seems safest under the mattress. And realizing that no matter what the government does they are bound to upset one group or another, bureaucrats retreat to that age-old wisdom: why stick your neck out when you can go home at 5:30?

While Hong Kong struggles to dig herself out of the rut, China is busily grooming Shanghai to dethrone her as the region's financial hub. After all, the politburo has had it up to here with our shenanigans. Crybabies in Hong Kong are constantly pushing the envelope with their calls for political reform and testing Beijing's short supply of patience. The only reason the hard-liners haven't yet sent in the tanks to flatten our hilly island is because of that other island across the strait. If Hong Kong is the father's annoying daughter, then Taiwan is no doubt the estranged wife who left the old man after a bitter divorce in 1949. In this dysfunctional family, the big sister is nothing but a decoy for the father to lure the divorcée home for a happy reunification. Back when the Basic Law, Hong Kong's mini-constitution, was still being drafted, Beijing figured that 50 years should be plenty of time for Taiwan to reconcile with the Mainland and it stamped an expiration date on Hong Kong's semi-autonomy: July 1, 2047.

13 years into the 50-year countdown, Hong Kong remains the only place on Chinese soil where dissent of any kind is tolerated. Falun Gong (法輪功) practitioners, the No. 1 enemy of the state, hold daily congregations in busy Causeway Bay, complete with human cadavers lying on makeshift operating tables to reenact an organ harvesting scene in rural China. Every Handover Day on July 1, tens of thousands take to the streets to vent their grievances against the government and to push for political reform and universal suffrage, words that have long been erased from the Chinese language in the Mainland. Who could have thought that a money-grubbing, materialistic brat would turn out to be the goddess of democracy for the rest of China? In the tale of our city, it seems, there is no shortage of irony.

Hong Kong is a city of many contradictions. A single cough is enough to cause a panic in the elevator, and yet everyday we breathe toxic air into our lungs and shrug it off as a case of *c'est la vie*. Penny-smart shoppers who haggle over a catty of *choy sum* at the wet markets would not think twice before pouring their life savings into the stock market under little regulatory oversight. Hoping to improve their prospects, men and women spend precious evenings studying for the CFA and collect professional designations like baseball cards, but never once question a government that cannot see beyond its nose. Just as the streetcar will keep running and congee shops will stay open, day after day citizens get on with their lives as though all is normal, tacitly accepting the *status quo* as immutable and irrefutable. In the end everything stays the same but nothing stays the same, for we regress if we don't progress. But every once in a while, we surprise ourselves by snapping out of our existential sleepwalk, however temporarily, like those 150,000 quiet citizens who show up in Victoria Park every June 4 to commemorate the Tiananmen Square Massacre and remind us that there is still hope for the big sister.

Paradise of the Blind

Not long ago I asked a friend of mine what he thought about Vietnam. Lee, a Taiwanese living in Hong Kong, travels there frequently for business. "The country is not much to look at," Lee shrugged, "except for their beef noodle soups and mail-order brides." Indeed, there is a perception in the wealthier parts of Asia that, with all the human trafficking going on in the country, you can order Vietnamese girls online or even bid for them on eBay. My friend's candid response left me with a frozen smile and a broken heart. That's when I decided to write an article for all the Lees out there, not to change their minds but to open them to a beautiful country with an ugly past.

I visit Hanoi and Ho Chi Minh City, Vietnam's twin metropolises, a few times a year for work. Few in Hong Kong know or care much about Vietnam. To the average vacationer, the country lacks the exciting nightlife of Thailand, the sandy beaches of Indonesia and the must-see attractions of China and Japan. And in the eyes of the Hong Kong Chinese, Vietnamese culture is decidedly bland and derivative. After 1,500 years of intermittent occupation by imperial China, every aspect of its culture, from food and music to social customs and even the gods they pray to, was borrowed from the Chinese. If a nation's written language is a measure of its cultural prowess, then Vietnamese is certain to disappoint. Like Tagalog and Bahasa, Vietnamese is a spoken language that relies completely on the Latin alphabet and a dizzying suite of diacritics. No wonder the country remains something of a blind spot in Asia, the same way that Laos and Burma have fallen off our radar screens. Ignored and forgotten.

A street vendor navigating her way through an endless stream of motorcycles

Last month I took two back-to-back business trips to Hanoi. The capital city is not beautiful, its streets are run-down and the buildings in a pitiful state of disrepair. Throughout the city, bundles of frayed electrical wires drape precariously over pedestrians and motorcyclists. As always, I stayed at the Hilton Opera Hotel, so named because it is located next to the Hanoi Opera House, modeled after the Palais Garnier in Paris and one of the few vestiges of French colonial rule still standing in the city. Not long after the Chinese occupation ended, French gunships arrived and established a new colony called French Indochina in the late 19th Century. Despite their relatively short occupation – less than seven decades from 1885 to 1954 – French colonists left an indelible mark on the country's culture, political system and education, as did the English on Hong Kong and Singapore. To this day, the upper crust of Vietnamese society still send their children to France for a Western education and many of the privileged speak French instead of English as their second language.

My business meetings may have been a 10-minute walk from the hotel, but crossing the six-way intersection in a city that has neither traffic lights nor lane markers is no easy feat. Pedestrians must learn to follow their blind faith and wade through charging traffic at a steady pace. Slowing down, speeding up or stopping midway can have dire consequences. Dubbed "Motorcycle City of the World," Hanoi boasts the largest number of motorcycles per capita in the world. Legions of bikers swamp every street and alley, blaring their horns not out of safety but rather to exert their existence. Motorcycles made by Honda, Kawasaki and Yamaha are a testament to Japan's enormous business investments in Vietnam. In 2008, Japan's development aid surged to nearly US$1 billion, making it the single biggest country donor to Vietnam. Bringing cold cash and hot skills, the Japanese found their way back to Vietnam, nearly half a century after the immeasurable suffering they inflicted on its people during World War II. The half-decade invasion began with Emperor Hirohito's (日皇裕仁) "Vietnam Expedition" in 1940 and ended with two million deaths from war-induced famines. When the Japanese finally surrendered to the Allies in 1945, they left behind a power vacuum that would open an even darker chapter in the country's haunting history.

I finished my meetings for the day and hurried back to the hotel to change into a T-shirt and shorts. I grabbed my trusty Nikon and wide-angle lens, hoping to capture Hanoi's street life while I still had the sun. Here in the capital city, the *hoi polloi* make no bones about taking their daily activities to the streets: a friendly game of billiards or Chinese chess, a badminton match between mother and son, and even a haircut or a perm in the privacy and quiet of the dusty sidewalk. Everywhere you go you see children, teenagers and adults in their 20s, 30s and 40s, a glaring reminder that Vietnam has one of the world's youngest populations. Two decades of Vietnam War wiped out entire generations of men and women, punching a big hole in the nation's anthropology. From 1954 to 1975, the United States used the impoverished country as its battlefield to fight a not-so-Cold War against the Soviets and the Chinese. By the time Saigon (now Ho Chi Minh City) fell and American troops pulled out of the God-forsaken place in 1975, the destruction was complete. As many as three million Vietnamese soldiers and civilians lost their lives, and the indiscriminate use of toxic herbicides to defoliate the countryside – where many of the guerillas hid – left millions more suffering from dioxin poisoning and resulted in a complete collapse of the country's agricultural industry. The effects of these defoliants, including the infamous Agent Orange, are still being felt today. In the aftermath of the protracted war, hundreds of thousands fled the country in search of food and shelter. Many of these "boat people" found their way to Hong Kong, after the English conveniently volunteered their colony as a "port of first asylum" in the 1980s to showcase their world-class generosity.

Back at the hotel, I ordered a glass of red wine – an Australian shiraz – from the bar and munched on a bowl of cashews while I took in the surroundings. A table of Korean businessmen at the hotel café thumbed busily on their Blackberries. Further away, a pack of Mainland Chinese swaggered out of the Dunhill store with bagfuls of purchases, conversing in loud Mandarin that echoed through the marbled lobby. Three and a half decades after the founding of the Socialist Republic, Vietnam is no longer a closed economy isolated from the rest of the world. 1986 was a turning point for the nation's economy, as the Communist Party began its economic reform modeled after China's Reforms and Openness (改革開放) initiatives. Between 1990 and 2005, Vietnam consistently achieved a 7% annual GDP growth, making it one of the fastest growing economies in the world and the envy of neighboring Cambodia and Laos.

Everywhere in Hanoi, I can see fragments of the country's bitter past. The ghosts from its history, those haunting shadows of old intruders and the innocent lives they took, stare right back at me. Life has been unkind to Vietnam, prayers to their gods unanswered. Just the same, the people journey on, despite and perhaps *because* of the sullen memories they share. Through its struggle and survival Vietnam reveals its true beauty, a beauty expressed not in shapes or colors, but in dignity and strength. To my friend Lee or anyone else who sees only with their eyes, the country is patently poor, dull and undeserving of our attention. But to those willing to close their eyes and open their hearts, it is an iridescent celebration of the human spirit. I finally understand why Doung Thu Huong, renowned Vietnamese writer and political dissident, titled one of her early novels *Paradise of the Blind*. And I will title this article with the same.

Nikko Revisited

It has been eighteen years since I last visited Nikko (日光), an idyllic city nestled in the mountains of Tochigi Prefecture (栃木県) two hours from Tokyo by train. My memories of the city have yellowed, but time has only made the heart grow fonder. And so when I decided to spend Chinese New Year in Tokyo this year, I made certain that a proper visit, long overdue, was paid to the City of Sunlight.

I planned a three-day sojourn at a *ryokan* (旅館; traditional inn) in the town of Kinugawa (鬼怒川). A popular *onsen* resort in the city of Nikko, the town was named after the Kinugawa River, which literally means the wrath of demons. Far less sinister than its name suggests, the sleepy town is home to thousands of retirees eager to chat up visitors who cross their paths. At the *ryokan*, a moon-faced *kimono*-clad attendant received me, bowing and smiling constantly. I was led to a one-bedroom suite comprising a generous ten-*tatami* living room complete with a wood decked patio, a Western-style bedroom and an in-room hot bath. I smiled back to the hostess in total satisfaction. Thoughtful as it is, the foreigner-friendly bedroom is a needless appendage, as the traditional futon mattress spread over *tatami* flooring offers a far more authentic *ryokan* experience and is always preferred.

I dropped off my luggage and slipped into a *yukata*, not a moment too early for an evening dip in the coveted *rotenburo* (露天風呂; outdoor bath). At the hot spring, silky steam rose steadily from the surface and guided the obeying eye through the surrounding garden. A Japanese pine leaned gracefully against a line of leafy shrubs and a stone lamp stalwartly stood guard, all draped in a thin coat of mid-winter snow. The scorching water tested my mettle, making every inch of skin crimson like the cheeks of a bashful child. As my body slowly adjusted to the temperature, the faint smell of sulfur and gentle whispers of lapping water took over my senses. Suddenly, the evening clouds gathered and began to drizzle. Frosty raindrops danced noisily all around, providing a welcome reprieve from the *onsen*'s unyielding heat. I took a deep breath and submitted to the whims of nature, dissolving powerlessly in her cradling arms.

Dinner awaited me at a private dining room. A twelve-course *kaiseki* (懐石) meal was a perfect act to follow the hot spring's pampering. Each day the resident chef designs the *menu du jour* based on fresh offerings from the local markets and creates a feast as much for the eye as it is for the stomach. From the elegant assortment of *sashimi* to the steamy king crab *sukiyaki* and the handspun *soba* served cold, each course is an edible work of art that balances the taste, texture and colors of carefully chosen ingredients and combines *haute cuisine* with local flavors and seasonal themes. Too beautiful to eat and too delicious not to, it was a dilemma of the best possible kind.

I spent the next day visiting the obligatory sites in the main city area, starting with Toshogu (東照宮), a Shinto shrine dating back to the Edo (江戸) Period, and ending with that long-standing symbol of Nikko, the scarlet-colored Shinkyo (神橋) wood bridge. Each place was exactly the way I remembered them, except they all seemed to have shrunk in size over the course of time. I suppose things in our memories are always larger than life. As I retraced my steps through the mountain paths, each bend and turn stirred up blurry images of my school friends and me running up and down the slopes snapping away with our clunky film cameras. Back then, we dismissed the *onsen* as an old people's pastime and skipped it entirely. We rushed through the *kaiseki* dinner in successive gulps before running off with our flashlights for a scavenger hunt in the nearby forest. We were teenagers then, with too much energy and too little patience. Such were the careless, happy days.

The famous Shinkyo wood bridge in Nikko

I spent another night at the *ryokan* and ended my sophomore visit to Nikko the following day. On the train ride back to Tokyo, I was once again struck by the quiet beauty of the mountain-bound city. Eighteen years apart, my visits to Nikko past and present made for two very different trips, taken at two very different stages in life. Like having re-read a favorite book, I was overcome by a wonderful sense of rediscovery.

沒有摩天大厦的城市

City Without Skyscrapers

Every year around April or May, I spend a weekend in Taipei doing absolutely nothing. With hardly any tall buildings, the flat, sprawling city inspires the kind of magnificent laziness best described by the Italian phrase *dolce far niente* (literally, sweet doing nothing). Each time I visit Taipei, I immerse myself in good company, good food and that trademark Mandarin spoken with a soft, disarming, if not altogether seductive accent where every other sentence ends with the lilting syllable "uh" (嗯). I also make an obligatory visit to a famous herbal medicine shop in the Ximending (西門町) area, where I atone for my filial impiety by getting my mom a year's supply of *ba xian guo* (八仙果), a traditional throat lozenge made from sun-dried chayote that she swears by and stockpiles in her pantry. "You can't find such potent throat medicine anywhere else in the world but this one store in Taipei," my mom reminds me all the time.

*　　*　　*

Nicknamed "treasure island" in the Chinese world and "Formosa" (literally, beautiful island) by the Portuguese, Taiwan is an idyllic, resource-rich island. About the size of Maryland, the speck of land has long been the target of territorial conquest by world powers. Since the 17th Century, colonizers from the Dutch and the Spanish to the Chinese and the Japanese came and went, until the *Kuomintang* (國民黨) fled Mainland China after the Chinese Civil War ended in 1949 and founded a new republic on the verdant island. Ever since then, Taiwan has led the existence of a renegade island, spending billions every year lobbying around the world to regain its seat at the United Nations and assert its sovereign status. So far Taipei has made modest progress by trading foreign aid in exchange for diplomatic ties with several small island states in the South Pacific and a handful of impoverished countries in Africa and Latin America. Across the strait in the Mainland, unification of the two republics to end a 60-year divorce has always been the Communist Party's biggest obsession and only mandate. Much to America's delight, China's messy personal life provides Washington enormous leverage over more pressing issues such as balance of trade and North Korea.

During the post-war period, Taiwan successfully transformed itself into an export-driven economy through a combination of monetary and land reform policies, state-owned enterprises and economic aid from America. In the 1990s, the country clinched the title of microchip capital of the world and became one of the leading exporters of smart-phones and laptops. Unbeknownst to many Chinese people, Taiwan's rapid economic ascent has much to do with imperial Japan which snatched the island from Qing China after a pivotal, humiliating naval upset in 1895 that ended the First Sino-Japanese War (甲午戰爭). Right from the start of its annexation of Taiwan, Japan showed remarkable benevolence toward its colony. The Meiji (明治) court promised equal treatment for Taiwanese and Japanese nationals under the *doka* (同化; assimilation) campaign and set up a modern, corruption-free government that ruled the local population for more than half a century. Even during the post-independence period in the 1960s and 1970s, Taiwan continued to ride on Japan's coattails by supplying parts and cheap labor to its former colonizer and benefited enormously from its rising hegemony in the consumer electronics and automobile industries. That explains why many in Taiwan, especially the older generations who have lived under Japanese rule, show gratitude and nostalgia toward Japan for modernizing their nation and giving them the education and governance they needed to stand on their own feet. The dynamics between the colonizer and the colonized were not dissimilar to those between the British and the Hong Kong Chinese.

*   *   *

I arrived in Taipei last Friday evening and checked into a boutique hotel on Chongxiao Road (忠孝路), the main artery that runs east-west and bisects the capital city neatly into north and south sections. Other than a handful of tourist hotspots like the National Palace Museum and the Chiang Kai-shek Memorial Hall (中正纪念堂), there isn't much to see in Taipei. The absence of impressive architecture and picture-worthy monuments is in fact part of the city's charm, as it takes away the pressure to rush from one sight to the next and gives me plenty of time to simply enjoy Taipei for what it is: a laid-back, friendly and very livable city where the rich offering of local delicacies and snacks is matched only by the warmth of its citizens. The fact that the city itself looks like Tokyo in the 1970s and that there are barely any skyscrapers other than the lonely Taipei 101 does nothing to deter me from returning year after year.

As always, I began my day with lunch on Yongkang Street (永康街). A hole-in-the-wall noodle house, tucked in a dizzying warren of small alleys, serves up a beef noodle soup so delicious the street is now synonymous with the folksy dish. To walk off the carbs from lunch, I trekked six kilometers westbound on Chongxiao Road to City Hall Plaza and spent the entire afternoon at the eight-story Eslite Bookstore (誠品書店) nearby. Opened in 2006, the flagship store is the largest bookstore in Taiwan and carries over a million titles. The Chinese history section alone made me salivate like a kid in candy store and gave me one more reason to look forward to an early retirement.

Predictably and delightfully, my evening ended with a scrumptious dinner at Din Tai Fung (鼎泰豐), rated one of the world's top ten restaurants by *The New York Times* and for good reason. Foodies from far and wide visit the restaurant for its signature crabmeat dumplings, but it is my personal favorite, the red bean dumplings that blush like peonies and melt like butter in my mouth, that makes me go back time and again. Although Din Tai Fung now boasts many locations around the world, I only trust the original restaurant on bustling Xinyi Road (信義路) to deliver both quality and authenticity. When it comes to dumplings savory or sweet, it seems, I am every bit as particular as my mom is toward her lozenges.

The world famous Din Tai Fung *on Xinyi Road*

Whenever I am in Taipei, the subject of how the average Taiwanese thinks of us Hong Kongers always comes up at the dinner table. Surely we are known for our ambition, efficiency and worldliness. But for every compliment there is a honest criticism that still stings no matter how many times I hear it from my Taiwanese friends. There is a longstanding and perhaps well-deserved perception in Taiwan that Hong Kong people are crafty, cut-throat, materialistic and often times arrogant and rude. As much as I try to brush off the litany of unflattering adjectives as necessary qualities to survive in a big city like ours, I can't help but wonder how many among us in Hong Kong are aware of our image abroad and whether our bad rap is the price we all have to pay for our fancy skyscrapers.

This essay is dedicated to J. Chang.

I Heart NY

I

The regional jet made a hairpin turn over Manhattan before touching down at La Guardia Airport. It was a visual feast to end an otherwise uninteresting flight from Toronto to New York. At 5,000 feet, office towers in every shape looked like young sprouts shooting from the ground, competing for light. The silver spire of the iconic Chrysler Building shimmered gloriously, its beauty matched only by the mélange of red, orange and yellow that was the changing foliage in Central Park. My heart felt an immediate magnetic pull – I was home.

I left New York in 2005 to take up a job in Hong Kong, ending my six-year stint in a city that has comfortably held the title of Capital of the World for nearly a century. To defend my own title as a "Noo-Yawker," I make every effort to go back at least once a year, invariably around Thanksgiving or Christmas when the city is most irresistible. The Big Apple holds a special place in my heart: it was there I began my career as a corporate lawyer and spent many a sleepless night on deals that wound up on page 3 of *The Financial Times*. Surviving New York was as much a personal ambition as it was a necessity, and in the process I came to understand what it was like to fall in love with a city. It had me at *wassup*.

Manhattan is the crown jewel among the five boroughs that make up the City of New York. The Brooklyn peninsula, like Kowloon, plays second fiddle to its island sister superior in every way. The Manhattan-Hong Kong analogy is complete once you consider how Manhattanites can go through life without ever crossing the East River to the "dark side" but the reverse can never be said about their counterparts in Brooklyn.

Manhattan's topography is elegant in its simplicity. The phallic island is made up of twelve avenues slicing through its length from north to south, while 130-some "cross-town" streets connect the west end to the east. The most prominent exception to this perfect grid plan is Broadway, a thoroughfare that runs diagonally through the entire island, creating interesting six-way intersections that became such landmarks as Columbus Circle, Times Square and the Flatiron District.

After dropping off my luggage at the hotel, I hopped onto the "V" train to visit my brother in Chelsea. Many big metropolises are defined by their public transport system and New York is no exception. The 105-year-old New York subway, the largest in the world, is every bit as idiosyncratic as the riders who love it and loathe it with equal intensity. With 26 crisscrossing train lines (there were only three in Hong Kong until recently), the NYC subway system is a Gordian Knot for out-of-towners but fodder for lively debate among New Yorkers. If ever one person is asked to give directions, everybody will jump into the fray and offer a different permutation of connecting trains.

Back in my commuting years, I braved the elements waiting on the air-conditionless platform, watched rats as big as household cats scamper off with their finds and had my ears split every time those old clunkers rumbled violently down the tracks. But as the quirky *New York Times* columnist Alice Rawsthorn aptly pointed out, the familiar subway signage printed in clean, crisp Helvetica typeface is a comforting sight that makes up for all that dirt, noise, smells and delays.

Shopping is a national pastime in New York and the department store is the playground of choice. From the venerable Bergdorf Goodman, Barneys and Saks Fifth Avenue to the more mass-market Bloomingdale's and Macy's that occupy entire avenue blocks, these New York institutions are at once sanctuaries and animal traps for the Carrie Bradshaws among the citizens. In a city of shopaholics, even grocery shopping has been elevated from a household chore to an art form. Gourmet markets like Dean & Deluca, Whole Foods and Citarella pop up on every street corner, any of which would make our own City Super look jejune. The mere process of picking through beautifully arranged organic vegetables is therapeutic in its own right, but what one actually does with the ingredients is not nearly as important, considering that a true New Yorker never ever cooks.

My favorite kind of shopping, however, is far less glamorous: buying used books. On any given weekend, I could spend an entire afternoon rummaging through old shelves, climbing up and down those Jacob's ladders to literary heaven at Strand's, a megastore that boasts 18 miles of books. Or I would walk into the dreamy, otherworldly Argosy Bookstore on 59th and Lexington and walk out with an out-of-print title or a vintage map fallen out of a half-century-old atlas. Moments like that made happiness seem just a little more within reach.

But no account of Gotham City is complete without mentioning its hyperactive restaurant scene. I pride myself as the walking *Zagat's* (a survey of over 3,000 restaurants published annually under its signature burgundy-colored cover) among friends. At the top of my list is Bouley in the swanky TriBeCa area. Fitted with vaulted ceilings and a foyer full of fresh MacIntosh apples, the restaurant is a playroom for celebrity chef David Bouley to experiment with nuanced, thoughtful culinary concoctions. *Prix fixe* dinner for two at these "all-caps" restaurants — so called because their names appear in all capital letters in the *Zagat's* for their popularity — would set you back around US$300, steep by any standard but still far better value than most over-priced hotel restaurants in Hong Kong.

Empire State Building adorns the island of Manhattan

The following morning, on my way to a business meeting in Midtown, I passed by Rockefeller Center where workers were busy putting up a gorgeous 80-foot tall Christmas tree. Distracted by the wholesomeness of it all, I inadvertently stepped on something mushy on the sidewalk. I looked down and there it was, a giant dead rat lying prostrate between my dress shoe and the cold asphalt. Passers-by looked but did not slow down, neither a wince nor a gasp. I lifted my foot off the roadkill, rubbed my sole off the curb and continued my walk down 51st Street. It was a classic New York moment. In the City that Never Sleeps, everyone has places to go and people to see. The good, the bad and the ugly — New Yorkers have seen it all. That is why we love New York.

II

New York is not America. It is what America wants to be, minus the 45.5% income tax and the 15% gratuity at restaurants.

In much the same way, Hong Kong is not China but what China should be, minus the air pollution and corporatocracy. But Hong Kong and New York have a few more things in common. For starters, worker bees in both cities pay exorbitant rent to live in a tiny apartment with barred windows looking right into someone else's home. Everyone takes public transport and many never bother to get a driver's license. Single women lament the scarcity of eligible men and rush to tie the knot before they hit their sell-by date, while men cling to their bachelorhood like koalas to a eucalyptus tree. Above all, both cities take great pride in their gutsy, razor-sharp and sleep-deprived citizens who, in trying to improve their own lives every day, create a better tomorrow for everyone else.

That explained why I hardly needed any adjustment to my repatriation to Hong Kong. But where there are similarities between the two cities, there are also jarring differences. Whereas Hong Kong is pulling all the stops to keep Shanghai and Singapore at bay, New York remains unchallenged at the top. And being at the top has its perks: New Yorkers exude a self-evident confidence, the kind of inner strength that perhaps few in Hong Kong understand, let alone possess. Much of a Hong Konger's self-worth, on the other hand, seems to come from what we wear on the outside: the Rolex on our wrist, the Porsche in our garage and that powder-blue Hermès Birkin handbag we finally get our hands on after being on the wait list for nine months. This also explains why New Yorkers tend not to judge a book by its cover. The middle-aged jogger in the ragged college sweatshirt may very well be the CEO of a Fortune 100 company. The waitress at the diner down the block may become the next Julia Roberts a year from now. Here in Hong Kong, where material things still impress, a pretty cover is often all that the book has going for it.

A century after unseating London as the world's financial hub, New York remains the Big Apple that promises a bite for everyone. Whether it is art and entertainment, professional sports or high finance, you haven't quite "made it" until you have proven yourself here. New York is where the *crème de la crème* in every field from every corner of the world converges. The moniker "New Jerusalem" is therefore as poetic as it is fitting. And therein lies another striking difference between New York and Hong Kong: diversity. Hollywood has given us ample examples of the menagerie of characters that roam the city's streets, from the neurotic Alvy Singer in Woody Allen's *Annie Hall* to the street rat Enrico "Ratzo" Rizzo in *Midnight Cowboy* and the mock-naïve faux-socialite Holly Golightly in *Breakfast at Tiffany's*. New Yorkers may be all of those things or none of those things, but you can bet they don't all watch the same soap opera and spend Saturday nights at the same karaoke bar the way people do here in Hong Kong.

New Yorkers are notoriously icy, cynical and sometimes downright rude. Their austere façade is part of a collective effort to keep out the faint of heart and separate the men from the boys. But once the newcomer has shown the moxie to stick it out, he is certain to discover a bounty of warmth and generosity from his fellow citizens, as well as opportunities he has never seen before. This Darwinian model was what drew me to New York in the first place and what eventually drove me away. In time I realized that as long as I stayed there, I would always be a small fish in a very big pond. As much as New York is an ideal training ground to hone skills and test mettle, the trainee must one day graduate from the city and return to wherever he is from – Houston, Frankfurt or Shanghai – and be that big fish in a right-sized pond. That's why most who pass through New York stay there for only a few years. And that's why I decided to leave the Big Apple four years ago.

The 9-11 attacks forever changed New York. What happened on that fateful morning took away the city's innocence and the nation's sense of security. I was on a southbound "2" train to lower Manhattan when the first plane hit the North Tower. After being evacuated from the subway, I made an 80-block trek up 5th Avenue alongside tens of thousands of citizens-turned-refugees. Traffic came to a complete halt; shoes and empty baby-strollers strewed the silent streets. Apocalypse had befallen the city. Though the steel structures have crumbled, the strongest steel of New York, as it was once said, has always been in the spine of its people. Surely enough, the city picked itself up and displayed admirable resilience and grace. Neither a terrorist attack nor the biggest economic crisis since the Great Depression can faze this unfazable city. The famous lines from Frank Sinatra's *New York, New York* sum it up well:

> *These little town blues are melting away*
> *I'll make a brand new start of it in old New York*
> *If I can make it there I'll make it anywhere*
> *It's up to you, New York, New York*

尋
覓
漢
城

Seoul Searching

I

I snatched the ream of documents from my secretary's hands and shoved them into my carry-on luggage. And so began the 48-hour cycle of a mundane business trip: a mad rush to the airport, a hurried nap on the humming plane and two days in a faceless city. Far from the glamor its name suggests, business traveling these days is all business and hardly any traveling. Imagine a trip where the final destination is a stuffy conference room and your travel companions a table of men-in-black who take their jobs way too seriously. Outside the dreary meeting room and just minutes from the sterile office building, a city beckons, waiting to be discovered. For an avid traveler like myself, it is the adult world equivalent of leaving a child behind the iron bars of the Disneyland entrance gates. So close, and yet so frustratingly far away.

This time my Mission Uninspirational took me to Seoul. Most of us in Asia know the capital city by its former name, Hanseong (漢城), after the legendary Han River (漢江) that bisects the city into two halves. Gangnam-gu (江南區), the southern half, is decidedly more affluent than the north and is home to scores of swanky bars and clubs where local yuppies see and are seen. But outside that insular area, unseen and impenetrable to the passing business traveler, Seoul is dated in its appearance and lacks the character and presence of a world-class metropolis. Visitors are also hard pressed to find much else to do in the city other than eating and drinking. To put another nail in the coffin, the six-century-old Namdaemun Gate (南大門), one of the city's very few points of interest, was torched by a 69-year-old arsonist last year. All in all, Seoul falls short of a capital city befitting a country that boasts the world's highest broadband Internet access per capita and hosted a summer Olympic Games and a World Cup.

The Sinocentric Chinese would tell you with pleasure and pride that all Koreans are descendants of Chinese settlers and that the Korean culture is completely derivative of the Chinese, from language and philosophy to art, music, cuisine and martial arts. The latter claim has much truth to it, as the country formerly known as Goryeo (高麗) did import its customs wholesale from Ming China before infusing them with its own sensibilities. The Korean language, for instance, is written in *hangul*, a phonetic alphabet invented in the 15th Century but not universally adopted until the 1950s. For centuries Chinese characters or *hanja* (漢字) were used exclusively in official documents and among the literati and social elite. Even today, *hanja* continue to figure prominently in literature and artwork and to cure ambiguities in homophonic *hangul* words in the print media. All students in South Korea are required to memorize hundreds of *hanja* in school, although most will forget everything as soon as they walk out of the classroom; everything other than the three characters that make up their own names.

The decline of imperial China in the late 19th Century put an end to Korea's cultural import from the Middle Kingdom, and the falling out between the two nations was further complicated by the bloody Korean War in the 1950s. But despite the ideological and political divide, the two peoples continue to share one thing in common: their grudge against Japan's genocide in World War II. Between the mass murders of civilians and the two hundred thousand "comfort women" (慰安婦) forced into sexual slavery by the Japanese military, the unsettled score between Korea and Japan is appalling, complex and still very much alive. It is in this national enmity that South Korea and Communist China become uneasy bed-fellows, joint in their outrage against the glaring omissions of war atrocities in Japan's history textbooks and the occasional visits by Japanese statesmen to Yasukuni Shrine (靖国神社) where a handful of Class-A war criminals are honored.

These days, much of the country's anti-Japanese sentiment gets vented through international sporting events, as the battlefields shift to soccer stadiums and ice-skating rinks. In the 2002 World Cup co-hosted by the two sworn enemies, South Korea became the first Asian country to ever make it to the semi-finals. The history-making achievement was sweet, but showing up the Japanese in front of 1.5 billion stunned viewers around the globe was ecstasy. And the South Koreans knew how to repay a favor. Guus Hiddink, the head coach who led the national team to its unprecedented success, became the first-ever foreigner to be bestowed the country's honorary citizenship and received sizeable financial rewards, not to mention a private villa on Jeju-do Island (濟州島) complete with a life-size statue of the Dutchman himself to honor his contribution to a grateful nation.

As the sun set lazily on the Han River, my plane touched down at the Incheon International Airport, rated best in the world every year since it snatched the coveted title from Hong Kong in 2006. Alone in my hotel room perched atop the peaceful Mount Namsan (南山), I took in the panoramic view of the sprawling city before me, lost in a moment of reverie. Then suddenly my eyes refocused and caught sight of the carry-on luggage reflected in the dark window pane, lying still on the turned-down bed and coldly reminding me of the all-day meeting starting promptly at 8 o'clock the next morning. I heaved a sigh of dismay and began to unpack, accepting the unavoidable. Although my interest in the Korean culture does not come close to the secret obsession I harbor for all things Japanese, I embrace it with a healthy doze of curiosity. And while the Korean people do not quite endear me the same way as do the Thais and the Taiwanese, I find them passionate, driven and positively quirky. Those were enough reasons for this keen observer to embark on a defiant quest to seek out the city's many idiosyncrasies. And so began my journey of Seoul searching.

II

It was 12:05 pm and we were still on item 2.3 of the two-page agenda. Inside the conference room as white as a morgue, bankers and lawyers pored over company accounts and peppered senior management with probing questions prefaced with profuse pleasantries. Jin-hoon, my colleague and friend, faithfully translated every word for me like a seasoned UN interpreter. Then came the first piece of good news of the day: we were to break for lunch in 15 minutes at a nearby restaurant. *Kamsamnida*, I whispered the only Korean word I knew despite myself.

Outside the office tower, the midday sun had warmed the urban sprawl to a balmy 25 degrees. Lunch-hour traffic crawled through the concrete veins, a stately Hyundai *Equus* here and a nimble KIA *Cerato* there, but not a single foreign car in sight. It was pocketbook patriotism in the most visible form. On our way to the restaurant, Jin-hoon and I traded thoughts on the recent suicide of former president Roh Moo-hyun (盧武鉉). Politics is a national pastime here and the sensational story of a change agent for South Korea falling from grace has set the nation abuzz. Roh's shocking suicide has completely shifted public perception of him, from a political piñata to an instant saint. His life and death make for a real-life soap opera that gives television epic *Dae Jang Geum* (大長今) a run for its money.

But few realize that Roh was only the fourth democratically elected president since the country emerged from a military dictatorship in 1987. Just months before she walked onto the world stage as the proud hostess of the Seoul Olympics in 1984, South Korea was still mired in political turmoil and paralyzed by nationwide protests demanding democratic reform. A failed Olympics in front of the watching world would have brought great shame to the entire nation, and that risk was enough to force army general Jeon Du-hwan (全斗煥) out of power and result in the watershed June 29th Declaration promising sweeping political reform. Those who had hoped that the Beijing Games in 2008 would bring about similar changes in China must have been sorely disappointed.

At lunch, we crouched around a long mahogany table not twelve inches from the *tatami* floor and covered with umpteen tiny dishes of *banchan* (飯饌). The company secretary who sat next to me, Mr. Son, told me that he spent six months studying the Chinese language in Shanghai several years ago. I listened with interest and initiated a friendly Mandarin conversation. Mildly embarrassed, Mr. Son confessed that he had forgotten most of what he had learned, but he looked to his seven-year-old daughter, now taking Chinese lessons every Sunday morning, to do him proud. Mr. Son's story of transferred dreams reminded me of an article I read in the newspaper that same morning: the story of 18-year-old skater Kim Yu-Na (金妍兒) who had just won the gold medal at the 2009 World Championships. The skater, now an A-list celebrity in Korea, owes her success to an unrelenting mother who devoted her entire life to making a superstar out of her child. Kim's mother quickly became a role model for every parent in Korea, her bestselling memoir an instant parenting bible. In a country known for parental dedication, high-achieving children are at once a pension plan, a ticket to happiness and the only way to keep up with the Kims and the Parks.

Back in the conference room, the meeting droned on. I struggled to stay awake with all that *kimchi* and *myeolchi* (dried anchovies) gurgling in my stomach. Three shots of coffee, two bathroom breaks and five more hours of due diligence later, we finally decided to call it a day. I packed my briefcase with unconcealed excitement and bade farewell to company management with a 90-degree head bow. Jin-hoon and two of his office buddies offered to take me out for dinner at Cham Sut Gol, a well-known *gogi gui* (barbeque) restaurant. Dinner is where Korean salary men blow off steam over grilled meat and alcohol. Lots and lots of alcohol. On any given night, men in groups of five or six, their faces redder than a ripe tomato, totter out of wine bars and threaten passers-by with gastric trajectories. Knowing full well what I was getting myself into, I gingerly accepted Jin-hoon's dinner invitation and braced for a night of liver assault.

On our way to the restaurant, we passed by the burned-down Namdaemun city gate, boarded up for reconstruction and drenched in the golden glow of the setting sun. Near the gate, a crowd of university students congregated, laughing and teasing each other. They were a far cry from the violent anti-government protesters I used to see on the evening news when I was a child. I told Jin-hoon that those were my earliest images of South Korea: fearless teenagers throwing petrol bombs at riot police. With a tinge of melancholy, my friend explained that those street protests are now a thing of the past, thanks to the 1997 Asian financial crisis. The crisis hit Korea particularly hard and threw entire classes of university graduates into unemployment, leaving them with student loans and injured pride. While studying abroad, Jin-hoon and many of his compatriots had to quit school to go back to Korea as their parents could no longer afford costly tuition. A comfortable future no longer assured, university students in the post-1997 era returned to the classroom from the streets and traded activism for a middle-class existence. Reality bites, and in this case, also silences.

At the dinner table, the four of us talked and laughed, eagerly topping up each other's glasses before they were emptied again in chivalrous gulps. We talked about everything and anything, from the rampant male chauvinism in Korean society to the mass weddings of the Moonies. But it was the topic of the *ajuma* (middle-aged married women) that drew the most laughs and got everyone nodding and stumping their feet. Nicknamed the "third gender," these visor-wearing, umbrella-wielding women in their 40s and 50s with the same hairdo as Kim Jong Il (金正日) are tough, ferocious and never to be messed with. Jin-hoon and his friends regaled me with their own impersonations of the *ajuma* screaming at her husband or a street punk. By 11:30 pm, I was lying prostrate on the *tatami* floor, exhausted from laughing and unable to move after washing down two pounds of beef with gallons of beer, *soju* (燒酒) and *bokbunjaju* (覆盆子酒), a black raspberry wine that tasted just like port. I was one drink away from becoming a red tomato myself.

A pack of ajuma *taking a break in a park*

My mundane business trip in Seoul turned out to be unexpectedly rewarding. My quest to explore the city went no further than a couple of short trips to nearby restaurants, and still I managed to walk in the shoes of a Korean salary man for a day and catch a glimpse of a people shaped by a storied past and united in a collective pursuit of a better nation. Over the span of five decades, the country went from virtual anonymity to a leader in technology and pop culture, thanks to a government that sets goals for itself and 50 million committed citizens that make them happen. The country's undoubted success has left Hong Kong's bureaucrats scratching their heads wondering how the Koreans did it. It must be something in the *kimchi* they eat.

Bangkok Story

I

I hopped on to the purple-tailed Boeing 747 and let Thai Airways whisk me away to one of my favorite cities in Asia. Just a little over two hours from Hong Kong, Bangkok is a ready playground for vacationers of all ages. A passport and a change of clothing were all I needed for a three-day getaway. For everything else, there was the credit card.

March and April are the hottest months in Bangkok but that was little deterrence to this ardent visitor. As soon as I stepped out of the new airport designed by celebrated architect Helmut Jahn, the familiar tropical heat wrapped around me like a thick, damp blanket. Using my hand as a visor, I looked up at the cloudless sky and squinted at the blazing sun bearing mercilessly down on the capital city. Like a frightened animal, I scurried into the hotel car before the first sweat broke.

As usual, I started my weekend "mall-hopping" in the Chit Lom area along Rama I Road. The activity is much less banal than it sounds. Shopping centers are a microcosm of society and sauntering through the megamalls in Bangkok provides a window into Thai society from riches to rags. My walking tour started with the ritzy Erawan and Gaysorn, twin shopping centers that are frequented only by deep-pocketed foreign tourists and local socialites. But the recent political unrest that unfolded in the capital city has taken its toll and left the marbled buildings with one empty floor above another. Further west down the street, the mid-market Siam Paragon was swamped with the country's burgeoning middle class. Moving in a slow eddy, women sampled the latest cosmetic inventions, while men peeped into new models at the in-mall car show. Thai people sure love their skin-whitening products and automobiles. I ended my tour at the low-end MBK Center and Siam Square, both buzzing with local teenagers and bargain hunters. Outside the shopping centers and along the filthy alleyways, panhandlers and impoverished migrant workers stared unseeing at the pedestrian traffic that passed them by, reminding freewheeling shoppers that income disparity remains a social issue that is very much alive in Thailand.

If Hong Kong has its air pollution and Tokyo its xenophobia, Bangkok's greatest woe is its notorious traffic jams. That afternoon I made the regrettable mistake of taking a taxi from my hotel in Chit Lom to the Nana area, turning a mere 10-minute walk into an hour-long involuntary confinement in the backseat of a diminutive taxicab. At the Rama IV and Phaya Thai intersection, the traffic lights refused to turn green for a full five minutes, trapping traffic from all directions and making one wonder how a capital city could function with such inefficiencies. The BTS, an elevated transit system that opened less than a decade ago to tackle the city's traffic congestion, has so far delivered little of its promise. It has been as much a city-planning blunder as it is an urban monstrosity. Enormous concrete structures supporting the train tracks hover above the main arteries of the city, casting a permanent shadow on all human activities down below and defacing an already architecturally uninteresting city.

Despite the country's imperfections, every Thai person, rich or poor, loves their country and adores their king unreservedly. Twice a day, the national anthem is played on every television channel and radio station. At any given movie theater, the audience rises to their feet before the show begins to sing the national anthem and praise the king in unison, a phenomenon that both bewilders and endears.

Back at the hotel, I lay by the poolside for a quick tan while the bartender poured me a mean lemongrass martini. A dissonance of jackhammers and metal saws from a nearby construction site pierced the tranquility. Resilient as ever, the city continues to grow despite the global recession. But Bangkok too has seen its fair share of calamities. It was only a year ago that anti-Thaksin protestors took over the city's two international airports, holding the tourism-driven economy hostage and threatening to throw the country into anarchy. Political instability, fueled by the eternal problems of income disparity and widespread poverty in the countryside, continues to stand between Bangkok and the world stage. But as any Thai person would tell you, in the depth of a sweltering summer, only patience and *jai yen* (literally, a cool heart) would bring positive change to their beloved country.

II

I visit Bangkok three or four times a year. Surely the food and the shopping are great and the hotel suites and health spas are to die for. But truth be told, I go there in large part because I like being around Thai people. Gentle, patient and friendly almost to a fault, the Thai are natural born hosts and hostesses. With these proud national traits, Thailand has carved a niche for itself as one of the top, and certainly the most pampering, travel destinations in South East Asia.

Thai people are also remarkably creative and artistic, qualities that are often overshadowed by their hospitality. The country leads the region in interior design as well as avant-garde fashion. Thai pop music, little known outside the country, is unostentatious and heartfelt, a welcome alternative to Hong Kong's formulaic Cantopop. Much of its magic is attributed to the Thai language itself. Spoken by over 65 million people, the tonal language is distinctly melodious. When addressing elders, colleagues and strangers (including tourists such as myself), the speaker ends every sentence with a soft *krub* (if the speaker is a male) or *kah* (if the speaker is a female), a syllable that is often sustained to produce an almost nagging sound, making the conversation all the more endearing and soothing.

Bangkok has some of the region's best healthcare professionals and private hospitals, and the city is quickly becoming Asia's top destination for medical tourism. Some of my expat friends in Hong Kong regularly visit Bangkok for routine physical exams and less urgent medical needs. Three years ago, while visiting a friend in his new office, I hit my head on a glass wall and ended up with seven stitches above my left eye. With blood gushing down my face, I was rushed to a nearby emergency room that dispensed world-class medical care at a fraction of what I would have paid in any major city. Later I found out that the doctor who treated me was Ivy League educated, which explained why he spoke perfect English to me while sewing me up.

Thai Prime Minister Abhisit Vejjajiva greeting reporters with the wai

Whenever I am in Bangkok, I play the harmless game of tourist identification with my friends. Over time I have become rather good at it. With tourists visiting from every corner of the world and each group exhibiting distinct idiosyncrasies accentuated by the tropical heat, the temptation to play detective and put cultural stereotypes to the test is irresistible. The real challenge, however, is to make up your mind before the target gets within earshot, at which point his accent would reveal the answer. Canadians and the Japanese are among the easiest to identify. The former never travel without their obligatory backpacks with the maple leaf flag sewn or pinned on it, whereas the latter bury their noses in their colorful guidebooks and love taking pictures of the food they order. Then there are the Americans who go everywhere in cargo-shorts and flip-flops and are quick to compare everything they encounter to its counterpoint back home; the Russians, ever sweaty and disheveled, seem to be bumping into people wherever they go; and the Germans never eat anything without a glass of wine or a beer can in hand and ask an inordinate amount of questions.

Among the many nationalities, Hong Kongers are the most interesting to pick out. Our tourists are decidedly rough in their table manners, talking loudly with their mouths full and pointing their cutlery at each other. Some of them act aggressively toward the soft-spoken, non-confrontational locals, barking orders as if the entire country were their live-in maids at home. In fact, many in Hong Kong still see Thailand as an impoverished third-world country where prostitutes and transsexuals roam the streets looking to make a quick buck. In trying to exert their superiority over the locals, these *jai dam* (literally, black-hearted) visitors end up insulting themselves and shaming their own kind.

Respect, patience and tolerance are among the many cherished virtues in Thai culture. Everywhere you go in Bangkok, people greet you with a polite *wai* gesture, a bringing together of the hands with the thumbs placed just below the mouth – though the higher the hands are held in relation to the face the more respect is shown. I enjoy giving and receiving this graceful form of greeting whenever I am in Thailand and find myself doing it even in Hong Kong when thanking someone for a favor. There is a great deal for all of us here to learn from this respectful and respectable people.

III

Last month I took a trip to Bangkok for work. It was right around the time when anti-government protestors began entering the capital city to open yet another chapter in the country's bloody political history. Frequent visitors to Thailand such as myself have long grown accustomed to its political crises that ebb and flow roughly on a biannual cycle. At best, Bangkok is an epicurean paradise where foreign vacationers and the local working poor pass each other by on the streets like ships in the night. At worst, the city is always one political misstep away from becoming the epicenter of the next social upheaval, military coup and inevitable bloodshed.

And so it started all over again on the hot, breezeless March day when a recent Supreme Court decision to seize the assets of former Prime Minister Thaksin Shinawatra triggered mass demonstrations by an army of 100,000 Red Shirts. Inside the Grand Hyatt Hotel where I stayed, I spotted Hong Kong reporter Addie Lam (林子豪) and his cameraman sitting in the lobby café busily going over their plan of attack to cover the half-dozen demonstration hotspots across the capital city. Outside the hotel, at the normally bustling Erawan intersection, armed soldiers replaced the usual afternoon crowds. Like animals that could sense the coming of a monsoon, local Bangkokians had all but vanished from the streets. Khun Gap, a friend of mine from my old law firm, canceled dinner with me because he had already left the city to spend a few days with his relatives in a nearby town. Although storm clouds were gathering, there were no signs of panic or chaos anywhere in the city. Here in Thailand, political instability is both a force of nature and a fact of life. And in the eyes of seasoned Bangkok citizens, the latest follies orchestrated by Thaksin loyalists were a mere inconvenience to be shrugged off with a "*mai pen rai*" (loosely, "oh well").

When it comes to mobilizing crowds, the Thais have taken a page from Taiwan's political playbook: color-coding party affiliations to minimize confusion and maximize visual impact. The practice began in the 2006 military *coup d'état*, when supporters of the anti-Thaksin People's Alliance for Democracy (PAD) wore yellow to symbolize their loyalty to the king, whereas followers of the pro-Thaksin National United Front of Democracy Against Dictatorship (UDD) chose red for courage and determination. But regardless of the color they put on, Thai protestors are much more hired guns than true social advocates. Every slogan-shouting, noisemaker-rattling Red Shirt we saw on the evening news was simply another peasant bused into the city to take part in a political show staged and financed by the UDD. Men and women from the poor northern provinces, hired at less than a few hundred Baht a day, got a free trip to the city, square meals served in Styrofoam boxes and a little extra cash in their pockets to take home. That would explain why many Red Shirts appeared festive and even jovial despite the serious political demands on their lips.

"Rent-a-crowds" are nothing new in emerging economies. A Filipino friend of mine once put the going rate for a full-time demonstrator in her country at 150 pesos (US$3.40) a day. There is even a "price list" for more newsworthy behavior such as getting a bloody nose from riot police or throwing oneself in front of a moving vehicle. This is a point that the foreign press so often misses. Just today I heard NBC's news anchor Brian Williams call the anti-government insurgence a "struggle over democracy." In reality, there is nothing ideological about these mass demonstrations. The Red Shirted protestors are simply pawns in the chess game between a billionaire ex-PM and the ruling elite who dislike him. In this modern-day reenactment of a Greek tragedy, the Titans clash but they bleed the blood of the poor. Admittedly, however, it would take more than a few hundred Baht and a free bus ticket to get otherwise happy peasants to risk their lives on the sooty streets of Bangkok. The truth is, there is plenty of unhappiness to go around in Thailand's rural hinterland these days. To put things in perspective, half of the country's 39 million labor force is in the agriculture sector toiling away daily in rice paddies and on fishing boats. Despite all the prosperity that the rapid economic growth during the Roaring Decade – from 1985 up until the Asian financial crisis – has brought the nation, power and wealth remain in the tight grip of the establishment. The widening income gap between the haves and the have-nots begets a deep sense of resentment among the grassroots majority living outside the handful of big cities.

Enter the Obamian leader, current Prime Minister Abhisit Vejjajiva. Young, handsome and charismatic, the Eton- and Oxford-educated Thai-Chinese is himself the product of the aristocratic gentry. The latest anti-government movement placed the pedigreed PM right in the center of a political quagmire. On the one hand, giving in to the UDD's demands to dissolve parliament and call new elections would mean losing everything that the Abhisit administration had worked for since he came to power two years ago. On the other hand, letting these shenanigans drag on any longer would further frustrate the public and weaken the already fragile economy, not to mention the irreparable damage to the young PM's own credibility. Dispersing the Red Shirts by force would also be tricky business. One false move and the military-backed government could have a Tiananmen Square on its hands. To make things worse, King Bhumibol Adulyadej, the "guard of the people's power" who normally gets the last word in any political conflict, is too frail to play arbitrator any more. If the 82-year-old king did not take a stance in the 2008 crisis that saw the removal of former Thaksin-friendly PM Samak Sundaravej, he certainly wasn't going to do it this time.

Until this weekend, both the Red Shirts and the government had exercised considerable restraint. Neither side wanted to upset the delicate balance of a standoff or give the other side an excuse to go to Plan B. But in an abrupt move that dashed all hopes for a peaceful resolution and exposed Abhisit's lack of control over military hard-liners, the government sent in the army to clear the streets. Batons, bullhorns and pick-up trucks finally gave way to tear gas, hand grenades and armored vehicles. The month-long standoff spun out of control and the so-called "Black Saturday" left twenty dead and hundreds more wounded. The worst side of Bangkok was once again on full display, those unmistakable images of third-world bloodshed and anarchy.

Island Escapade

小島偷閒

I grabbed my carry-on luggage and headed out of the office at lunch time. An in-flight movie and two rounds of drinks later, I found myself at the island airport greeted by a smiley hotel chauffeur reminiscent of Tattoo from *Fantasy Island* — minus the white suit.

I had booked myself a private villa on a remote Thai island overlooking the South Pacific horizon. The spacious one-bedroom suite, complete with its own infinity edge pool, a teakwood patio deck and a verdant landscaped lawn, was to be the perfect setting for a weekend getaway.

At least that's what I thought when I planned the trip several weeks ahead of departure. Things began to go awry when anti-government protesters besieged Bangkok's two main airports and, one by one, countries around the world issued travel advisories against Thailand. Then came the gloomy forecast on weather.com that there would be a 90% chance of a thunderstorm every day during my stay at the resort. Oh well, I said to myself, and pressed ahead with the original plan.

A sandy beach at a Thai island resort

Things didn't turn out nearly as grim as I had expected. The island was sunny for most of the weekend, and the outdoor temperature registered at a comfortable 26 degrees. A ginger dip in the pool, however, proved the water still too cold for a swim and I opted for the lawn chair, watching the ocean waves hit the sandy beach. As the frothy whitecaps traveled ashore, the symphony of tides crescendoed to a climax, persuading me to surrender to its powerful sway. The cosmic harmony engulfed and released, bombarded and caressed, in perfect undulations that calmed the nerves and soothed the soul. Not to be upstaged by the turquoise sea, the tropical sun pierced through clustered clouds and bestowed upon me a coat of bronze that would never go out of style. Cradled in the arms of nature's two most powerful forces, I felt my energy renewed and my zest for life rekindled.

"What more can I ask for from a vacation?" I thought to myself, eyes shut and head nodding.

一年後的東京

Tokyo Impressions – A Year Later

When it comes to men's clothes, there isn't much in Hong Kong to choose from besides European and American imports. In the advent of "vanity sizing" that caters to those ever-expanding waist lines in the West, foreign labels have one by one sized me out over the years. And so I turn to Japan, where the local demand is strong enough to support ready-to-wear clothing made just for the petite Asian man. Where else can I pick up pants with a 29" waist off the rack season after season?

A few weeks ago I found myself back on the bustling streets of Shinjuku (新宿) and Shibuya (渋谷) to catch the tail end of the winter sale. I raided the usual hotspots, checking off my shopping list and day by day filling up an empty suitcase. As always, I made a conscious effort to do as the Tokyoites do. I burrowed through the underground colony of the subway system, scoured the city for best-value restaurants and unwound after a day of shopping in front of the television while munching on a panoply of over-packaged snacks spread across the bed, all the while keeping a close eye on a city that never ceases to fascinate me.

The night I arrived a few Japanese friends took me to a *yakitori* joint in Roppongi (六本木). The restaurant was touted as a mecca for salary men from the glitzy financial district nearby, but I wouldn't have guessed that myself. At 7:45 on a Thursday evening, we were one of only three tables in the sleepy restaurant. Since I first noticed the disappearance of long lines from the Tokyo restaurant scene a year ago, the global recession has all but strangled the life out of the capital city. Lavish after-work drinking shindigs have given way to a new consumer behavior: save up during the week and spend it all on the weekend. But no matter how hard the economic downturn has hit, a sliver of Japanicana remains firmly entrenched. Across the restaurant at the corner table, a man in his fifties clad in a black trench coat – an old cog in the corporate wheel – droned on about Japan's revolving-door prime ministers and interjected his diatribe with a lewd joke or two. Next to him a pair of younger men blushing from warm *sake* responded to the sexual innuendos with 45-degree nods and air-sucking sounds. A lone female associate refilled everyone's cups in circular motion before offering her own witty repartee to the boss's off-color remarks. "Some things never change," said one of my friends, a skilled eavesdropper, after he translated the entire conversation for my dubious benefit.

The next day I spent the afternoon in Shinjuku's Sanchome (三丁目) area. No shopping spree in Tokyo is complete without a proper visit to Isetan Men's, an eight-floor, shop-till-you-drop megamall dedicated to dressing up the metrosexual male. On each floor, store clerks tailgate stoic customers and impart intelligence gathered on the *dernier cri* in menswear, all part of their charm offensives to reverse the sharp fall in consumer spending. The twin evils of a shrinking population and rising unemployment continue to widen Japan's demand gap and threaten the economy with a vicious circle of deflation and negative growth. But when the going gets tough, the tough get going. This time around every purchase I made at the cashier was met with even bigger smiles and deeper bows. At the Paul Smith store, the young sales clerk was so happy I finally decided to buy a jacket that she forgot all her training in *keigo* (敬語; honorifics) and exclaimed in unbridled excitement, "oh really? Thank you, thank you, thank you very much!"

At 9 pm, the metal gates began to come down at the Odakyu and Lumine department stores that flank the Shinjuku train station. The squeaky sounds of the unrolling aluminum were cues for the dozen homeless people to begin their nightly routine. Men in their 40s and 50s appeared out of nowhere and meticulously set up makeshift tents using cardboard boxes and newspapers. A rice ball from a nearby Lawson convenience store and a cup of hot tea made for a scrumptious dinner in tough economic times. Nowhere is Japan's recession more evident than in the bowels of the city: under a dusty overpass, on the landing of a fire escape stairway and along the stretch of covered ground outside every train station.

After dinner, my friends joined me in the hotel room for a nightcap. We watched a news file on TBS, one of Japan's major television networks, as I packed for my day trip to the outskirts of

Tokyo the following day. It was the story of a university graduate who solicited donations on the Internet for a living. While still talking to the reporter, Koji – for that was the name of the cyber panhandler – received a ¥5,000 deposit in his PayPal account from an anonymous donor in Osaka. If the young man is any indication of Japan's Generation Next, then the Lost Decade of economic stagflation is all but certain to carry over to the next generation. Lacking the sense of purpose that gave their baby-boomer parents a secure middle-class life, the Kojis of Japan are mounting a retrograde movement against the socio-economic structure of post-war Japan. Not exactly the kind of thing that an aging society needs.

Homeless people camping out on the sidewalk

My shopping weekends in Tokyo double as a Japanophile's social study field trips. Every visit I have made since the global recession bears out the suggestion that the superpower is on an epic decline. China has recently unseated Japan as the world's second-largest economy, while South Korea is soon to replace it as the cultural trendsetter in Asia. Earlier this year, JAL, Asia's biggest airline and a longstanding symbol of the venerable *kabushiki kaisha* (株式会社; stock company), filed for bankruptcy protection and threw a third of its workforce into unemployment. Toyota, Japan's largest corporation that accounts for over 5% of the country's GDP, announced a series of massive recalls that threatened to topple the 73-year-old empire. Company scion Akio Toyoda (豊田章男) apologized for his products' deadly defects at a two-day House hearing in Washington, D.C. last week. The world looks on, wondering whether the Rising Sun is all but certain to fade into the twilight. But if Japan's lack of political leadership, the burst of its asset price bubble and an economy that depends too heavily on infrastructure spending are all contributing factors to its epic decline, then let that be a lesson for us all in Hong Kong.

Jason Y. Ng

As I See It

Visit the author's online column today at
www.jasonyng.com